HOW WILL THEY HEAR IF WE DON'T LISTEN?

HOW WILL THEY HEAR IF WE DON'T LISTEN?

RONALD W. JOHNSON

BROADMAN
& HOLMAN
PUBLISHERS

Nashville, Tennessee

© Copyright 1994
BROADMAN & HOLMAN PUBLISHERS
All rights reserved
Printed in the United States of America

4210-67
0-8054-1067-8

Dewey Decimal Classification: 248.5
Subject Heading: WITNESSING // EVANGELISTIC WORK
Library of Congress Card Catalog Number: 93-36219

Unless otherwise noted, Scripture quotations are from the Holy Bible, *New International Version*, copyright ©1978, 1978, 1984 by International Bible Society.

Library of Congress Cataloging-in-Publication Data
Johnson, Ron, 1949–
   How will they hear if we don't listen? / Ron Johnson.
      p.   cm.
   Includes bibliographical references
   ISBN 0-8054-1067-8
   1. Evangelistic work.   2. Listening—Religious aspects—
Christianity. 3 Pastoral psychology   I. Title.
   BV3793.J614   1994
   269'.2—dc20   93.36219
                                                      CIP

To my mother and father—
W. O. Johnson and Grace Johnson—
Who always had time to listen to me
and who taught me God's love
by example and by their words.

CONTENTS

PREFACE

This book is about ministry—specifically, the ministry of listening. And it is about evangelism. At first blush the two disciplines may seem far apart, at opposite ends of the religious spectrum. This is because many hold to the idea that evangelism is first and foremost an activity based upon telling. That is, we tell people how to be saved. And listening is more a function of pastoral care, of helping to heal people. I believe the two can be merged in a natural relationship.

There are hidden problems with the idea that evangelism is *exclusively* a process of speaking to a person with little real dialogue taking place as the gospel is presented. And there are problems with listening and trying to offer healing without dealing with a person's primary illness, that of lostness. I hope to show in this book that we can actually learn to tell the gospel to others more effectively as we practice the art of care through listening to them—listening to where they are in life, hearing their questions, their doubts, their hurts, their goals in life, and so on. Only when we know what people are dealing with down deep in their innermost selves can we know how to effectively focus the gospel to their individual situations so that real healing can occur.

This is what Jesus did. He focused on the roadblocks to people's faith in God: a rich young ruler who loved money, a woman at a well who sought self-esteem through men who used her, and a ruler of the Jews who came to Jesus by night, seeking additional information about the kingdom Jesus proclaimed. Many other examples are in the Scriptures of how Jesus penetrated the souls of men and women as He talked to them, listened to their concerns, and showed them how to know the Father. Such is the need for today.

Many laypersons want to exercise a caring ministry of evangelism, but they are put off by the model of impersonal, high-pressure, confrontative telling. Yet evangelism does not have to be done that way. It can be done with great sensitivity. Among the caring evangelists that I have known through the years and who have mentored me in my personal witnessing are those people who know how to listen to others and then apply the gospel to their lives in specific ways that meet the deepest needs of that individual.

Learning to listen as a part of our telling the gospel is a challenge because we are people who have been trained almost exclusively in the art of monological presentation. I hope that this book will be an encouragement to many who will want to cultivate listening skills and then to apply them to a person about whom they care deeply, but who has been turned off by someone who has tried in the past to present the gospel to him or her without really listening to his or her felt needs.

This book is not a proof text for an escape from the necessity of telling others the good news of Jesus. Francis Du-Bose is right in saying that evangelism is proclamation in the mission of the church. In fact, learning to listen to people will enhance our proclamation. It will cause us to speak to them more often and in much more depth than we might otherwise do in our normal witnessing patterns. And learning to listen to others in order to tell them about Jesus is risky. It causes us to become involved in their lives, to answer a multitude of questions, to be willing to "make a defense to everyone who asks you to give an account for the hope that is in you, yet with gentleness and reverence" (1 Pet. 3:15). And it is hard work, for we become compelled to carry the burdens of people who are lost and to whom we listen. We pray for them often. They do not leave our thoughts when we know their life stories. When they come to Christ, we find joy in discipling them and mentoring them in the Christian life. And if they turn away from us, we feel what Jesus felt with the rich young ruler. We love them and we are saddened that they will not come to Christ.

Many people have written about relational evangelism. This book deals with building relationships with people. But what about those occasions when you sit beside someone on the airplane, or ride with someone in a taxi, or bump into an old friend in the supermarket whom you haven't seen in years? Can the gospel take root in situations where you do not have hours and days to develop relationships through listening?

The answer is yes. Listening can be done and done well over a period of days or in a few minutes of intensity. The point of this book is not the time period involved, but the process of taking the time to let the other person speak, to focus on her needs, and to provide answers based upon dialogue that centers in a gospel witness. I hope the book achieves this goal.

Many people have cared enough to encourage me to explore this issue in the book. I want to thank former colleagues at Southern Seminary in Louisville, Kentucky, where I taught for two years, for their support of me during a time when I was privileged to learn afresh new ways to listen to God and to discover His will for my life and ministry. Thanks must also go to new colleagues at the Georgia Baptist Convention, where I now serve, and to my administrative assistant at the Georgia Baptist Convention, Mrs. Peggy House, for her enthusiasm and long hours of reading the manuscript for the details of footnoting, proofing, and chasing down facts and figures.

And thanks must go to my family for letting me write while they enjoyed our vacation time together, and for letting me get up in the middle of the night, disturbing their sleep, to add ideas and thoughts to the manuscript over a period of many months of work. And thanks to you for reading the book. It is a first attempt to express my deep conviction that to make anyone else understand, we must be willing to first understand them.

Chapter 1

LISTENING TO TELL

What is the church's purpose in the world? The answer we give to that question cannot be based upon what *we* think or wish but rather must be fashioned in keeping with the purposes of its founder, Jesus Christ, and His mission for the church in the world.[1] His mission was God's mission from the foundation of the world—He was *sent* to do the will of the Father and to reconcile mankind to the Father. Francis Dubose has pointed out the significance of God's sending mission: "Of the some sixty references in John, almost all are theological, and some forty-four refer to the title of God as 'one who sends' and of Christ as 'one who is sent.' It cannot

---

1. Charles Van Engen, *God's Missionary People* (Grand Rapids: Baker Books, 1991), 92.

be overemphasized how deeply the sending concept relates to Jesus' identity."[2] Jesus expressed who He was in terms of His being sent into the world by God to redeem the world, to save mankind from sin.

MANDATE FOR EVANGELISM

The fact that the early church's creed proclaimed Jesus as Lord, the One sent from God, defined their position with regard to their understanding of His teachings. They chose to be under His command and authority. As such the early Christians had no trouble understanding the authority that lordship implied for them. They took seriously His words. They ministered because He told them to minister. They took seriously His mandate to evangelize their world, beginning from Jerusalem, because He told them to do so. It was His will.

Today, Christians have no less a mandate. Even so, many who call themselves Christians reject the mandate. This rejection is not so much a hostile one but rather rejection built upon the foundation of apathy, misinformation, laziness, or a poor understanding of the implications of lordship. These Christians have become victims of a kind of cheap grace through an easy believism. Instead of bowing to the lordship of Jesus Christ, as the early church did, many Christians have lapsed into a kind of progressive or evolutionary notion of lordship. These Christians believe that they can accept Jesus as Savior from sin and then, maybe later on down the road of faith, they will at some time make Him Lord of their life. What they do not understand is that this is rebellion of the most serious kind. Jesus is Lord. We do not make Him Lord. Rather, when He saves us, we submit our

---

2. Francis M. DuBose, *God Who Sends* (Nashville: Broadman Press, 1983), 49.

lives willingly to Him and to the knowledge that He is Lord—Lord of all!

One can hear the stinging message of Peter being preached at Pentecost, "Let all the house of Israel know assuredly, that God hath made this same Jesus whom ye have crucified both Lord and Christ!" (Acts 2:36). To fail to submit to Him as Lord of our lives is to depart from the biblical teaching and the early church's creed and practice.

Today this kind of easy believism, where all that is desired is release from the guilt of sin, with no real commitment to a radical change of life under the authority of Christ's command, has spawned a whole generation of so-called Christians whose behavior is indistinguishable from the rest of the unregenerate world. In a study of values among young people, one report stated that there was no significant difference between the moral values of Christian youth in the research sample and those of the sample from the secular world. The conclusion of the report warned that today's youth may be drawn into the quagmire of easy believism unless more is done to aid them in discipleship development.

"evangelism for many churches is not a passion but merely an additive or gimmick they sprinkle into the church program when church membership falls off. . ."

Our church rolls are filled with people who seem to have little or no real commitment to the things of Christ. They can become insulted when they are told that the gospel requires commitment to Christ's command for life. They do not want to hear words like "crucified with Christ" (Gal. 2:20); "the fellowship of His sufferings" (Phil. 3:10); or the fact that they must submit themselves to Jesus as Lord and

become like Paul, a "prisoner of the Lord" (Eph. 4:1). It is no
wonder many churches are so subnormal in their ability to
affect a lost and dying world. It is no wonder that evangelism
for many churches is not a passion but merely an additive or
gimmick they sprinkle into the church program when church
membership falls off. If church growth is ever to happen it
will be because persons are gripped by what it means to exalt
the Savior to His rightful place in their lives, homes, work-
place, and churches. Soul winning will no longer be a negative term for these Christians!

It is the lordship of Christ that must be our central creed
and fuel our passion for the lost, because "The lordship of
Christ drives the church outward in its proclamation of the
gospel to the world."[3] Because we know Him as Lord, we
desire for others to know Him as well. Our confession of
Jesus as Lord brings to us the understanding that such confession naturally drives us outward to all the nations. It is
good news, gospel, to be shared, not kept inside. "Therefore,
New Testament evangelism is in the finest sense a process of
communication"[4]—communication of good news.

Yet, many churches and many individual Christians are
quite content to declare Him Lord within the safe confines of
the Christian community alone, something the early church
knew nothing of. Harvie Conn has reminded us that "it
makes no sense for evangelistic proclamation to be made by
Christ's disciples only to Christ's disciples within the confines of the local church."[5] Conn goes on to say that the proclamation is only kerygmatic (essentially gospel) when it is
intentionally addressed to those who have not accepted Jesus
as Lord.[6] This is why we are engaged in evangelism.

3. DuBose, *God Who Sends,* 92.
4. Ibid., 117.
5. Harvie Conn, *Evangelism: Doing Justice and Preaching Grace* (Grand Rapids: Zondervan, 1982), 48–51.

Therefore, the central mission of the church is to point people to Jesus, to give them the good news of the gospel. As William Thompson has said, "The church of Jesus Christ is a worshiping and an *evangelizing community*."[7] That fact is not to be compromised. Evangelism is the process by which the good news is shared. While there are many definitions of evangelism and many methods, and while evangelism means many things to many people, the bottom line must be always evaluated by the faithfulness of the witness in sharing the gospel clearly with the lost around as to the best of our ability and as a result of our Lord's command.

OVERCOMING WALLS

Couched within the mandate to present the gospel to all mankind are several problems. One would think that such a simple thing as telling someone about Jesus would be easily accomplished. However, it is not. Obstacles are erected by Satan as he tries to dissuade us from our evangelistic mandate. And our own distinct methods, programs, and procedures used in getting the task done often present us problems.

One such problem has been the walls we sometimes erect based upon our way of looking at ministry and accomplishing the mission of the church. Why should there be a wall of separation between evangelism, missions, and ministry, for example? A goal of this book is to help begin the process of dismantling the walls separating ministry and mission from evangelism that may have caused some Christians to be hesitant in sharing their faith. It is my hope that, as a result of reading this book, the reader will catch the vi-

---

6. See also John R. Stott, *Christian Mission in the Modern World* (Downers Grove: InterVarsity Press, 1975).

7. William D. Thompson, *Listening on Sunday for Sharing on Monday* (Valley Forge: Judson Press, 1983), 13.

sion of evangelism as a ministry and sense even more the mission of God in sending us out to be witnesses of God's saving power within our lives. Christians should understand that God has given us both a mandate and permission to function with confidence as they share the faith with those who need to hear.

CATEGORIES

One of the strangest things westerners tend to do is to put things into nice, neat categories. Everything has a place. Everything should be in its place. Trying to put missions, ministry and evangelism into categories may be helpful for the way a church or denomination develops its program, but it surely confuses the issue when it hits the real world. A most striking example is how we have separated ministry from evangelism over the years. That should not be. To continue to do so will lead our evangelistic efforts into the trap of ineffectiveness, being less and less involved in the realities of life today. We can never be content to shout the gospel at people from a distance. Rather, we must, as Stott has said, "involve ourselves deeply in their lives, to think ourselves into their culture and their problems, and to feel with them in their pains."[8]

This dichotomy between evangelism and ministry has led to the weakening of both ministry and evangelism through the years. Denominational turf protection only exacerbates the problem. As the programs of various denominational agencies, state, and associational offices, filter down to the churches, the rift widens between mission, ministry, and evangelism. Ministers often see themselves as either mission-minded, evangelistic, or ministry-focused. Denominations appoint missionaries based on this dichotomy.

---

8. Stott, *Christian Mission,* 25.

Churches reflect this tension by describing themselves in their newsletters or on their church marquis as "A church that cares" or "A church where the gospel is proclaimed." Does the slogan imply that a church where the gospel is proclaimed is doomed to failure and insensitivity to ministry needs, or that a church focusing on ministry does not and is indeed hostile to the idea of presenting the gospel? The intention, of course, is to establish an identity—to build on natural strengths. But the message it gives to itself and the world is that the church approaches its task with one-dimensional thinking.

The assumption that ministry and evangelism cannot go together is due partly to the negative image of evangelism, usually propagated by television or radio evangelists and hucksters, or by some very negative experience that may have occurred when a person tried to share his faith but was rejected in the process. The fact that witnessing is something that most Christians have a hard time with is clearly portrayed in the churches where only a small percentage of Christians ever bother to share their faith with the lost in the course of a year. There are many reasons why Christians do not share: fear, lack of knowledge, shyness, busyness, and a host of others.

A woman who was over seventy years of age confessed in a witnessing class I conducted that she had never shared her faith. She went on to explain that she had been saved at the age of ten years and that she had grown up in a Christian home and in the church. She had served in the church in almost every capacity imaginable. She had been faithful in every program of the church. But in all that time she had never told another person about Jesus Christ. After the witnessing class was over she was so convicted about her lack of witness that she publically confessed to the church her lack of witnessing and pledged to begin immediately telling others about Jesus. Is she the exception? Research has shown she is the rule.[9]

This lack of evangelistic involvement by the average person in the pew is a serious matter for the church. Jacques Ellul is quite right when he says that the Christian has a part to play in this world which no one else can possibly fulfill. "He is charged with a mission of which the natural man can have no idea."[10] And that mission is to tell the lost about Christ.

Peter Wagner has optimistically stated that in the average evangelical church as many as 10 percent of the members have been given the gift of evangelism.[11] Wagner is careful to discriminate between the gift of evangelism, given to a few, and the fact that all Christians have the responsibility to witness. But it is one thing to suppose that some have been given the gift and something else to find whether or not the gift is being used.

If it is true, however, that evangelical churches have the potential of 10 percent of the members as evangelists, it would seem there would be more results in evangelism than we see. For example, if an average church had two hundred members with twenty members actively sharing their faith every week, surely we would see many additions to those churches in the course of the year.

Wagner's hypothesis was developed in the mid-seventies as a result of the observations he made of several growing churches like James Kennedy's church in Fort Lauderdale. Wagner goes on to point out in his book, *Your*

---

9. Ronald W. Johnson, "An Evauation of the Home Mission Board Program of Evangelism in Local Churches" (D. Min. doctoral thesis, The Southern Baptist Theological Seminary, 1988).

10. Jacques Ellul, *The Presence of the Kingdom* (Colorado Springs: Helmers & Howard, 1989), 3.

11. Peter Wagner, *Your Church Can Grow* (Glendale: G/L Publications, 1976), 76–77.

Church Can Grow, something that is very telling in his observation. He comments on the potential of ten percent of the members being evangelists by telling us, "if a church mobilizes the ten percent who have the gift of evangelist, and if these people win only one convert per year—a poor showing for a person with the gift—and bring that person into church membership, the church will triple every ten years."[12]

The key word that we must be careful not to overlook in Wagner's statement is the word *mobilize*. If there are 10 percent evangelists available to the churches, why is it that they are not being mobilized? In reality those who are mobilized are much less than 10 percent. According to some specialists, the number may be as small as one half of one percent of the average church membership! In fact, a recent news article suggested, "only four out of every 100 resident members of Southern Baptist churches led someone to faith in Jesus Christ last year."[13]

The Southern Baptist Convention presently boasts about 15 million members. Someone has cynically remarked that the FBI probably could not locate half of them. Are there 1,500,000 evangelists (10 percent) *mobilized*, on duty for God? If there are, then why are Southern Baptists only baptizing about 250,000 people each year from among the secular lost community?[14] Maybe Wagner is correct by stating that the evangelists need to be mobilized. Maybe all churches need to place a priority on *getting the ten percent moving!* And certainly we need to keep urging all Christians to take opportunities to share a word of witness in daily lifestyle.

---

12. Ibid., 78.
13. Quote from Howard Ramsey, director of the Southern Baptist Home Mission Board's personal evangelism department. Quoted in "Everybody Ought to Know, Evangelism Speakers Say," *Western Recorder* (March 3, 1992).
14. A baptismal analysis (total in 1992:367,847) will reveal that many baptisms are of our own member's children, from other denominations, rebaptisms and the like. The number baptized each year from the secular lost community varies, of course, from year to year, but remains around 250,000.

Almost all Christians know the Great Commission passage found in Matthew 28:19–20. (Some may be surprised to know that the Great Commission is also in Mark 16:15; Luke 24:46–48, John 20:21; and Acts 1:8.) And most know they ought to witness. Hence, many Christian laypersons and some pastors live with a nagging sense of guilt that somehow they are not doing what they know deep down they should be doing as Christians. Each time they hear a message on evangelism, a tinge of guilt surfaces. Often their intentions are good as they pledge to share their faith in the future. But many never get around to it. Why?

ENCROACHMENT?

One reason might be that evangelism is seen by some as encroachment. Evangelism has taken a very bad hit in the last decade. The reputation of the evangelist in some circles is that of harshness—cold and impersonal, only interested in the bottom line. In fact, authors have bent over backward to try to encourage people to share their faith without being harsh or insensitive.

A book by William George Harkey, published in 1988, even went so far as to admit the problem by suggesting that people learn *How to Share the Good News . . . Without Being Obnoxious About It!* Harkey explains in the book that some Christians have an easy time of sharing, while others cannot seem to bring themselves to do it. He sums up the problem common to the experience of many Christians:

> *You love your Lord, but you hate to witness. You can't quite understand it, but are aware that some Christians are eager to witness. Nevertheless, you cannot adjust to their styles. There are certain things you simply do not like. You notice that some Christian witnesses tend to be pushy. They violate*

others' privacy. They talk too much. You simply cannot accept this type of behavior. Nor can you change your personality to fit. God created you differently.[15]

Harkey goes on to tell us, "Millions of sensitive Christians, like you and me, are discouraged by the old methods. We find strong-arm witnessing at odds with society's needs."[16] The reputation of the obnoxious evangelist has spread to the point that some believe all who try to evangelize fit that mold! Does Harkey have a valid argument? A lot of people think so.

MEDDLING?

Evangelism is also viewed among many Christians as meddling in another person's life—judging her because of her lifestyle. A sense of inadequacy also adds to the mix. After all, a person may think, *Who am I to tell someone how they should confess their sins when I am so painfully aware of my own shortcomings?*.

"Can ministry-based evangelism become a reality in our churches?"

And evangelism seems so hard to do.

People believe that evangelism requires deep theological knowledge of the Bible or numerous memorized passages of Scripture in order to convince the lost that they should be saved. Many Christians just don't feel they have that knowledge—even those who have been in Sunday School

---

15. William George Harkey, *How to Share the Good News Without Being Obnoxious About It* (Lima: C. S. S. Publishing Co., 1988), 7.
16. Ibid., 19.

for forty years! This approach to evangelism is too hard for
a lot of people. But should evangelism be softer?

Ministry, on the other hand, is often seen as a softer,
more gentle approach that is warm and caring and that most
people, lost or saved, want to be a part of. Ministry, whether
carrying a food basket at Christmas to a needy person or
helping someone across the street, tends to make us feel
good about ourselves. Ministry identifies with humankind.
After all, each of us is in need of ministry at some point in
our lives and often on many occasions. Who hasn't had
tough times in life? It just seems natural to lend a helping
hand. Besides, there are all kinds of models around—volun-
teer organizations that minister, the Red Cross, government
agencies that help the needy, shelters—you name it. There is
an abundance of ministries going on. We see them on television everyday. So it is natural that churches and Christians
should want to be a part of ministry

A Possible Linkage

But is there a possibility that evangelism and ministry,
specifically personal ministry to others, might be joined in a
partnership that is authentic, warm, caring, and effective in
terms of sharing the gospel with lost people? Can *ministry-
based evangelism* become a reality in our churches? Can
Christians learn to listen in the marketplace to the life stories
of the lost? Can we respond in such a way that the need to be
saved is also included among the list of other needs such as
food, shelter, clothing, and so on, that call for attention in the
lives of the lost? Can pastoral ministry become sensitive not
only to a person's life problems but also their spiritual alien-
ation from God? Can the pastoral care minister learn to deal
with the clinical problems faced in the counseling session
and look for ways throughout the session to dialogue about a

person's greatest need of all—to be saved? Can the ordinary Christian become more pastoral as he deals with the lost?

LISTENING AND RESPONDING

This book addresses just such issues. It is a look at the ministry of listening and responding through dialogue as a legitimate evangelistic tool. Many of the old methods of the fifties and sixties don't work well today. Society has changed. There has been a paradigm shift in American culture away from the Bible belt value system toward a more agnostic, cynical, hostile, and violent system of values. Turn on the television and look at America. It is sexually permissive, foul in its language and extremely violent. As a result a whole new list of problems has surfaced that decades ago did not seem problematic.

In the fifties America was possessed of an optimism that promised its children: that cancer would be wiped out just as surely as polio was being wiped out; that industries would forever take care of their loyal employees; that there would be no more wars; that science would pave the way to a lifestyle of carefree leisure; that prosperity was there for anyone who would work hard to seize it; that education was the key to a future filled with promise.

Who would have thought that in the nineties the United States would be a debtor nation? That America would be moving toward a third-world status? That massive unemployment, AIDS, violence, global wars, and famine would be issues of the nineties? Who would have thought that the church would move from the center of society to a fringe position in most communities?

What happens if we go about our way, insensitive to the problems and issues of our day? If we fail to face the reality that the times are different? Is there a risk if we don't learn to listen to what people are dealing with today? Or if we think we know just because we observe the world through our eyes and make universal assumptions?

Approaching a witnessing encounter based upon wrong assumptions can put the whole process in jeopardy. "Top executives of a major technological company in the Midwest were asked recently to survey the role that listening plays in their work. Here are three typical comments made by participants:

Actually, I had never thought about the listening aspects of my work. But now that I am aware of it, I realize listening is one of my principal jobs, now I spend almost 80 percent of my time either listening to someone or having someone listen to me.

In reviewing the things that have gone wrong over the past two years, I realized that many of our snafus have been the result of someone not hearing something or getting it in a distorted way.

It's interesting to me that we've concentrated on communicating in this company but have inadvertently overlooked listening. I've decided that listening is one of the weakest but at the same time most important links in our whole communications network. We're not going to get anywhere until we learn how to listen better."[17]

The interesting thing about these comments is that these business persons have found they cannot effectively carry on their businesses without learning to listen, especially to the new issues of today. The risk of error is too great. If the secular business world is listening to others, how much more

---

17. Lyman K. Steil, Joanne Summerfield, and George DeMare, *Listening: It Can Change Your Life* (New York: Ronald Press, 1983), 4.

should we who claim to know Jesus listen to Him and to others?

Certainly the business of Christians is that of sharing Jesus with others. Yet, some may feel this approach, learning to listen to the life needs of people, is not direct enough, that it is somehow too anemic an approach to sharing the gospel, that the world needs to be confronted by our witness. One may well argue such a point. More will be said about this issue later on in the book.

But two things seem very clear in the experience of many who have learned to share the gospel inductively, from the point of human need. First, they have learned that Jesus did it that way. Jesus' evangelism was dialogical, it was situational, and it was servant-evangelism.[18] Second, they have learned "there is no such thing as an evangelizing community that does not listen to the world around it."[19] For these witnesses it is absolutely essential to let people tell their story, and in that process of dialogue, to interact with them regarding the gospel. But to clearly focus on how evangelism is enhanced by the listening process and through resulting dialogue one must define listening.

WHAT IS LISTENING?

Listening is more than just hearing. Listening is a proactive response. You have to get involved with another person really to listen to her. Perhaps this is a significant point to consider. How involved do we want to be in another's life? Jesus, as we shall see, knew how to listen to the real issues of life. He could bypass the words and listen to the heart. Christians today can do the same, if we will really learn how to listen carefully to the life journey of others.

---

18. Alfred C. Krass, *Evangelizing Neopagan North America* (Scottdale: Herald Press, 1982), 111.
19. Thompson, *Listening on Sunday*, 21.

How many times have you encountered a fellow worker at the plant and heard her tell the story of her family in turmoil? Or the teenager who tells you that she is frustrated because no one understands her? Or the senior adult who talks about the lonely days and nights he faces?

"Listening and its resultant dialogue may open new avenues for evangelism and careful ministry."

All around us, people are talking about their lives. Have you tuned into Oprah, Phil, Sally Jessy, et.al., lately? Sometimes we are sympathetic to persons' needs to share their life experiences. Sometimes we hear them speak and yet we cannot understand their pain. At other times we are too prone to compare our lives with their lives and perhaps whisper a thankful prayer that we have not been overtaken with their troubles or perhaps, in the worse case, to judge them. At best, we tell them we will pray for them. But often the words we speak are nothing more than just words. We care, but we are not sure what to do. If the person is lost, we may try to tell them about Jesus, but often they do not understand because they have not yet learned to live by faith.

Listening and its resultant dialogue may open new avenues for evangelism and careful ministry. Through listening the walls between ministry and evangelism may come down. They can be broken down as we learn to listen to the lost, to understand their lives, to respect them, to engage them in meaningful dialogue, to involve ourselves in their lives. Giving a cup of cold water, in Jesus' name, means not only helping to quench physical thirst, but helping quench spiritual thirst as well. And people are thirsty. . . just listen!

THINGS TO THINK ABOUT

1. EXPLORE THE CONCEPTS.

Think about the early church's proclamation of Jesus as Lord. In terms of your own witnessing responsibility, how does acknowledging Jesus as Lord affect your witness? What is your personal understanding of the Christian's mandate for evangelism?

2. SEARCH THE SCRIPTURES.

List as many Scriptures as you can find that deal with witnessing. List all the Great Commission passages. Commit them to memory.

3. DISCUSS THE PRINCIPLES.

In a small group or with a friend discuss some of the following issues: Overcoming walls. What are the walls in your personal life that need overcoming? In what category have you placed witnessing? Do you ever feel that witnessing is encroachment? How? Why? Is evangelism meddling in another person's life? How so? Analyze your listening skills at present. Are you a good listener? In what ways do you need help in listening?

4. ACT ON WHAT YOU HAVE LEARNED.

First of all, pray for God's Spirit to illuminate your thoughts. Second, Think of some specific actions that you can take this week to enhance your personal witnessing. Commit yourself to better listening this week. Ask someone to help you be accountable so that you will follow through on your commitments.

Chapter 2

IT'S A NOISY WORLD

Let the wise listen and add to their learning.

Proverbs 1:5

Try an experiment. Next time you are in a restaurant, a popular place of business, in a crowd, or just sitting on a park bench in the center of the city and eating your lunch, try closing your eyes. Shut out all the visual images. Rely on your ears the way unsighted persons have to . . . and listen. Just listen. Give it time. Listen for the loud voices, the soft voices, the pleasant sounds, the unpleasant sounds. Feel your ears react with loud sounds and with very soft sounds.

What you will find out, if you haven't discovered it already, is that we live in a noisy world. To put it more bluntly, we live in a world filled with ear pollution. I would imagine that while you had your eyes closed, you probably heard something that sounded quite interesting, but if the situation was normal the sound was interrupted by another sound that distracted you. And you lost track of what you wanted to hear.

Maybe it was someone whispering at the table next to yours in a crowded restaurant. Two lovers talking in a whisper about their honeymoon trip—interesting stuff. It even made you a little guilty, and maybe you felt like some kind of peeping Tom as you listened; nevertheless you listened. But right in the middle of their "I love you honeys," some clumsy waiter dropped a whole tray of glasses. The lovers probably looked away from each other for a moment, but my guess is that they kept on talking and listening to one another, maybe holding hands, lost in one another's eyes. But now you were startled. Your eyes opened wide, heart rate increased, and you were fully distracted, not able to keep up with what you were straining to hear. How often it is that the soft and beautiful gets trampled by the loud and ugly. It is hard to hear a bird sing on a busy downtown street. And it is hard really to listen in the midst of so much talking.

How we like to talk! Not long ago I visited a business that had installed a white noise generator to cover up all the noise generated in the office by people on telephones talking to clients, and workers conferring with one another desk to desk. Imagine that, a noise machine to cover up noise! A popular rock and roll song of the sixties lamented about a young man's girl-friend:

> *You talk too much, you worry me to death.*
> *You talk too much, you even worry my pet.*
> *You just talk, talk, talk.*
> *You talk too much.*

The average person can talk at a rate of between 175 to 185 words a minute. And when they get agitated, some people can talk at rates of three to four hundred words a minute. The world record is held by Steve Woodmore. According to the *Guinness Book of World Records*, he spoke an amazing 637.4 words per minute![1]

Obviously, talking is a central function of verbal communication. Some people are gifted orators. Who could forget Winston Churchill? His gift of oratory and inspiration coaxed millions of Britons through the dark nights of the *Blitzkrieg*. He encouraged his nation to rise up against the unthinkable atrocities of the Nazis and attain victory.

Churchill had the ability to weave words into powerful visual images. His words became the glue that held Britain together in their war against Hitler. For example, in a BBC broadcast on January 20, 1940, Churchill warned the British about the German plans for the future of Europe. While almost every other world leader was being wooed by Hitler, Churchill kept his resolve to warn of the dangers of listening to those who would put off action toward the threat:

> *All of them hope that the storm will pass*
> *before their turn comes to be devoured.*
> *But I fear—I fear greatly—*
> *the storm will not pass.*
> *It will rage and it will roar,*
> *ever more loudly, ever more widely.*
> *It will spread to the South;*
> *it will spread to the North.*
> *There is no chance of a speedy end*
> *except through united action.*
> *And if at any time, Britain and France,*
> *wearying of the struggle,*

---

1. Peter Matthews, *The Guinness Book of Records 1993* (New York: Guinness Publishing, Ltd., Bantam, 1993), 167.

were to make a shameful peace,
Nothing would remain for the smaller states of
    Europe,
with their shipping and their possessions,
but to be divided between the opposite, though
similar,
barbarisms of Nazidom and Bolshevism.[2]

Notice the poetic rhythm of his speech. No wonder he captivated his listeners.

Franklin Roosevelt's fireside chats proved to be a soothing balm to a nation in the midst of economic peril. Millions of Americans gathered around their radio sets to listen to the President. Many were so devoted to the weekly program that they hung his portrait near the radio so they could both see and hear their beloved leader. Some, like my grandfather, were so devoted to Roosevelt and his fireside chats that he willingly missed other programs on the radio during the week in order to conserve his battery-powered radio set for Roosevelt's speech. Both Churchill and Roosevelt had the ability to reach people in their homes and move them deeply through the medium of radio oratory.

OUR BASIC NATURE

Politicians, television personalities, radio disc jockeys, salespersons, and yes, even preachers make their living by talking.

Talking is basic to our human nature. The words we say are so important that Scripture warns us to be careful how we speak, that our words reflect our heart and that all of our words will be accounted for in the last day.

---

2. William Manchester, *The Last Lion: Winston Spencer Churchill* (Boston: Little, Brown and Company, 1988), 597.

"For out of the abundance of the heart the mouth speaks. The good man out of his good treasure brings forth good, and the evil man out of his evil treasure brings forth evil. I tell you, on the day of judgement men will render account for every careless word they utter; for by your words you will be justified, and by your words you will be condemned." (Matt. 12:34–37)

Matthew Henry commented on Matthew 12:34–37 by saying,

God takes notice of every word we say, even that which we ourselves do not notice. Vain, idle, impertinent talk is displeasing to God; it is the product of a vain and trifling heart. We must shortly account for these idle words; they will prove us unprofitable servants, that have not improved the faculties of reason and speech, which are part of the talents we are entrusted with. By thy words thou shalt be justified or condemned. The constant tenor of discourse, according as it is gracious or not gracious, will be an evidence for us, or against us.[3]

But what about the other side of verbal communication? How important is listening?

Actually, most of us listen more than we think we do. Out of the 70 percent of our waking hours verbally communicating, fully 40 percent of that time is spent listening.[4] If you are a student, you can actually spend over 57 percent of

---

3. Matthew Henry, *Commentary on the Whole Bible* (Grand Rapids: Zondervan Publishing House, 1961), 1267.
4. Madelyn Burley-Allen, *Listening: The Forgotten Skill* (New York: John Wiley & Sons, Inc., 1982), 2.

your time listening. Some estimates range as high as 90 percent of time that is spent listening if you are in a formal learning setting such as high school or college.[5]

But how we listen in the midst of a noisy world is what is so important. The more our schedules become crowded and the more demanding work becomes, the harder it is to listen effectively. We tend to develop a pattern of hearing that is just efficient enough to enable us to get along with the task we are performing or to satisfy us relative to some burning issue.

Eugene Raudsepp of Princeton Creative Research illustrates perfectly the problem of listening in a noisy world. He tells the story of a zoologist who is walking down a city street with a friend amid honking horns and screeching tires. He says to his friend; "Listen to that cricket!" The friend looks at him with astonishment. "You hear a cricket in the middle of all this noise?" The zoologist takes out a coin, flips it into the air, and it clinks on the sidewalk. A dozen heads turn in response. The zoologist says quietly, "We hear what we listen for."[6]

DISTRACTIONS

But some things are simply not worth listening to. One evening I was having a leisurely dinner after a hectic day of teaching, meeting with students, attending committees and the like. It was nice to be home and visit with my family around dinner. But you guessed it: the telephone rang. I took a sip of iced tea, sprinted to the phone, picked it up and said, "Hello." On the other end, momentary silence, then the tape began to roll and a computer voice came on saying, "Con-

5. Standford E. Taylor, *Listening* (Washington, D.C.: National Education Association of the United States, 1964), 3.
6. Lyman K. Steil, Joanne Summerfield, and George DeMare, *Listening: It Can Change Your Life*, (New York: Ronald Press, 1983), 9.

gratulations, you have been selected. . . ." I didn't wait to find out what I had been selected for. Instead I slammed down the phone and muttered to myself on the way back to my mashed potatoes. I resented the noisy intrusion into the peace of quiet conversation at mealtime with my family.

However, other things are very important to listen to. Amazingly, people usually do a very poor job of listening. Most of us are only about 25 percent effective as listeners.[7] I doubt if teenagers listen that much. I have three in my house.

Most parents can attest to the number of times they have had to exhort a young person to take out the trash or pick up his or her clothes. It is not enough just to hear sounds. Listening is an art. It has to be developed. We constantly have to learn to listen more effectively. That is why this book is about listening. People have to realize that we develop the art of listening. It is not a natural gift for most of us. It is important to learn to listen effectively for the sake of ministering to others—for the sake of our witness. Especially is it critical for those who would hope to become tellers of the good news.

More Than Receivers

Becoming a teller of the good news must imply more than just broadcasting the gospel in one direction toward people much like a radio station broadcasts music or news to a radio receiver. People are much more than just receivers of what we want to say. No doubt at some time in your life you have been forced to listen to someone preach, teach, or communicate with you using this model. If you are like most people, unless the speaker is entertaining, to the point, or a master orator, the whole process can be boring and dull.

---

7. Burley-Allen, *Listening: The Forgotten Skill,* 2.

Years ago communication theory taught us that we should use this sender-message-receiver kind of process. In other words, we told people what we had to say, and we expected them to hear and do. If they did not get the message, we simply looked for other ways to send it, or we repeated it over and over until they got it. That kind of process worked fairly well in a day when all teaching models were done that way, when society expected as much, and when the authority of the sender was respected. But today there are many ways to communicate, and respect for all authority has degenerated so that the sender-message-receiver model no longer works well.

Today, most communication theory advocates a transactional model. It is process-oriented. Various techniques are used to get the message across. It is often highly dialogical, for example.[8] Evangelism that would reach the secular person must be packaged in ways that enable him to hear. No longer can the evangelist have the attitude that what he is saying about Christianity is so compelling and so important that the world will naturally listen. It will not.

Many people have heard the gospel transmitted through the sender-message-receiver model for decades. And they have tuned religion out and tuned the world in with its exciting visual images and fast-paced music. Part of the challenge of evangelizing a world that has overheard the gospel is to create ways for people to really hear perhaps for the first time.

Robert Hughes advocates a receptor-oriented communication. He believes that we need to stop wasting energy trying to do the impossible—that is, passing judgement on what the world prefers to listen to, watch, and enjoy. Rather, what we must do is go to the world with quality communica-

8. From a lecture by Wally Buckner, Home Mission Board, SBC, given at The Southern Baptist Theological Seminary, 1992.

tion: conversation, books, tapes, movies, and the like. We must send messages to the world about our faith not based upon how they *ought* to hear, but based upon what we believe the secular listener is *prepared* to hear.

"The evangelist today must constantly remind himself that he is communicating in a world where the listener is used to silencing what he does not want to hear with the flick of a remote-control button."

The receptor-oriented communicator is sensitive to how the listener hears the message. He is aware of the way people listen today. He knows that the listener attaches meaning to the words he speaks. Therefore, he is concerned with studying the face of the listener to be sure the message is getting across.[9] He knows that if the listener is not watching and following the dialogue, no matter how beautiful the message is, it will be lost.[10] The evangelist today must constantly remind himself that he is communicating in a world where the listener is used to silencing what he does not want to hear with the flick of a remote-control button. Listeners today can turn off the message with ease. They know how to be selective. And they are not at all hesitant about being selective.

---

9. Robert Don Hughes, *Talking to the World in Days to Come* (Nashville: Broadman Press, 1991), 17.
10. Ibid.

Evangelism Defined

Evangelism has long been associated with proclamation or the simple telling of the good news. Donald A. McGavran and Win Arn in their book, *Ten Steps for Church Growth*, define evangelism in these words:, "to proclaim Jesus Christ as God and Savior, to persuade people to become his disciples and responsible members of his church."[11] Obviously, this is a sender-message-receiver approach.

The International Congress on World Evangelization, held in Lausanne, Switzerland, in July 1974, drew up one of the most important documents on evangelism that we possess. According to Delos Miles there is some recognition of the dialogical nature of evangelism in the document. Nevertheless, the Lausanne Covenant definition views evangelism proper as proclamation and persuasion.[12] We tell and tell until someone is persuaded and responds to the message. Such an approach reflects a simple design.

Deductive vs. Inductive Evangelism

Many people may not be aware of it, but evangelism is often defined under two broad categories. And witnesses tend to evangelize from two distinct approaches. One is deductive—beginning with the general and moving to the particular; the other inductive—beginning with the particular and moving to the general. Delos Miles has characterized the two approaches in his book, *Introduction to Evangelism.*[13]

11. Donald A. McGavran and Winfield C. Arn, *Ten Steps for Church Growth* (New York: Harper and Row, 1977), 51.
12. Delos Miles, *Introduction to Evangelism* (Nashville: Broadman Press, 1983), 40–41.
13. Delos Miles, *Introduction to Evangelism* (Nashville: Broadman Press, 1983),254.

These include:

Deductive vs. Inductive	
Receptivity (high)	Receptivity (low)
Monological (telling)	Dialogical (listening)
Short-term gains	Long-term gains
Canned	Spontaneous
Instant	Incarnational
Religious Persons	Secular Persons
Proclamation	Affirmation
Propositional	Point-of-need
Stereotyped	Service
Contact	Conversational
Functional	Friendship
Rational	Relational
Traditional	Target group
Individual	Household
Lips	Lifestyle

To characterize the two approaches as Miles does will lend understanding to the problems often encountered in witnessing. For example, people conceptualize differently. If a deductively oriented person is approached by an inductively oriented person, he may feel that the witness is never getting to the facts or that he is too "laid back." On the other hand if an inductive person is approached by one who presents the gospel everytime in a deductive manner, he may be turned off by the highly structured presentation of the facts.

According to Miles, the deductive style is tighter, quicker, more highly structured, employs "transferable concepts" which can be passed on immediately to other Christians, uses more religious language, requires more memorization, and so forth. The inductive style, on the other hand, is looser, longer, more flexible, less transferable, more secular, more spontaneous, and so forth.[14]

Deductively oriented persons like the memorized approach and the logical progression that witnessing plans and programs offer. Inductively oriented persons, however, tend to like those programs that establish credibility, that give persons creativity, and that give freedom to share in broad concepts. They do not react very openly to deductive approaches of the gospel nor to those who witness using that method. However, programs that are highly deductive have proved through the years to be very successful in leading great numbers from all walks of life to faith in Jesus Christ. We must be careful not to categorize one approach such as the inductive approach as valid and the deductive approach as somehow not as valid. Both have their place. And we should use both to bring people to faith in Christ. For some it will require structure. Still others live lives that will only be touched with a more inductive approach to sharing the gospel.

Understanding these categories is vital to helping people to be able to receive the gospel witness. However, it is just as vital that we understand lifestyle orientation.

---

14. Ibid., 254–256.

LIFESTYLE ORIENTATION

There are multiplied millions of Americans whose life-style is neo-pagan, agnostic, or secular. Tex Sample has identified three distinct lifestyles in America today. They are the Cultural Right, Middle, and Left.[15] These are not political, but lifestyle orientations.

Those persons belonging to the Cultural Right maintain strong traditional values. They respect family, flag, and America. Many of the cultural right are religiously-oriented persons, that is they understand the Bible as the sacred text, they understand church language, and hold traditional values respecting religion, even though many of them may not attend church. Many would define their lives around key, pivotal events that shaped much of their thinking, such as the Great Depression and World War II.

The Cultural Middle is driven by career. They are *strivers* hoping to make it in their career, *successfuls* who have made a good career, or *conflicted* who have had nothing but grief in the pursuit of a career. These persons can be very difficult to reach with the gospel because they are successful, or they are working seven days a week to become successful. Individualism is alive and well in the cultural middle. Those baby boomers the media has described as "Yuppies" can be found in the Cultural Middle.

The Cultural Left is made up of largely inner-directed, self-fulfilled baby boomers (some 33 million of them), though not exclusively. They tend to be committed to personal freedom and tolerance and committed to experiencing the here and now. They are often concerned about social issues and many are involved with New Age and other cults. Others in this group believe quite clearly that one does not have to go to church to be a good Christian. Sample asserts

15. Tex Sample, *U.S. Lifestyles and Mainline Churches* (Louisville: Westminster Press, 1990).

that the people in our society who are least likely to attend church are those on the Cultural Left.[16]

In all three lifestyle groups there are those who are religiously oriented and those who are not religiously oriented. For the religiously oriented church language makes sense. To those who are not religiously oriented, who are agnostic, secular, or neo-pagan, religious language carries little or no emotional or spiritual impact and is not easily understood. The witness must bear these issues in mind as he dialogues and listens to people in these categories.

Progress is being made as evangelists seek to understand not only lifestyle issues and religious orientation but also the deductive and inductive methods of witnessing. Some formerly deductive approaches now recognize the need to approach persons inductively in some cases. The 1977 edition of *Evangelism Explosion*, for example, included a long chapter on "The Gospel for the Secular Mind." According to Delos Miles, D. James Kennedy, and Archie B. Parrish learned from much experience that the standard EE approach was not reaching secular persons.[17]

More and more witnessing programs are surfacing that include the inductive approach. Even though the deductive method is somewhat difficult to use today with hosts of people, there are still times when it can be used effectively, especially with a person who has been raised in a religiously oriented environment and has a very high receptivity level toward the gospel. Those who are ripe for harvesting can often be approached effectively using a deductive method. Others, however, will take time to cultivate. Listening is definitely an inductive method. To understand more clearly how we often use the deductive approach in witnessing, a very

---

16. Ibid., 31.
17. Miles, 257.

generalized look at a common method of witnessing will be helpful.

THE DEDUCTIVE PROCESS

The normal pattern is to first secure a person who will listen to what you say. Sometimes this may be done by church members going door-to-door in a neighborhood during an organized soul-winning visitation night or stopping people on the street during the course of the day or even talking to a person in the seat next to you on the airplane.

Once a person's attention is secured, then the gospel message or "plan of salvation" is told to the person in a rather matter-of-fact way, often using a memorized presentation or a gospel tract or a marked New Testament. Finally, the person is asked to make a response to what he has heard, usually in the form of praying a model prayer. Generally, if the person agrees to pray a prayer along with the witness, the assumption is made that the listener has professed his faith in Christ. Most evangelical Christians probably realize that this is not the end but the beginning of a person's Christian life. Discipleship begins once the decision to trust Christ has been made. Often the witness then moves on to someone else. Many evangelists tell stories of success based on such a process.

But as Delos Miles points out, evangelism should not seek to convert persons merely through a once-for-all process. "Salvation in the Bible is more of a process than a once-for-all experience. Sin is ever present; therefore, there must be a continuous turning away from sin. Repentance is always needed. The Christian life is, in fact, a constant turning away from sin and setting our face toward God."[18] Therefore the

---

18. Ibid., 53.

witness must be careful to explain these concepts as much as possible within the presentation.

Instant evangelism, as Samuel Southard calls it, is an urgent and individualistic appeal for salvation.[19] The problem with this as Southard explains, is that "few if any questions are raised about the hearer's past, his present relationship to family and community, or his future hopes."[20] Dialogue is largely absent in the process.

There is another danger. Presenting a neat, well-packaged appeal to some people may indeed suggest to them that we know everything we need to know about how God chooses to work in the other person's life. We might unknowingly communicate a kind of arrogance as a result. Listening to people must transcend our expectations of them, our assumptions about what they need, our theological bias, and our desire for safety and control during the encounter. God may choose to work in a situation quite differently from what we have planned or expect. But we often insist on the comfort and security that a system brings, rather than to listen and wait to see what God will do in the witnessing process.

SYSTEMS

Perhaps it would be helpful to examine some of the popular methods that witnesses use in communicating the gospel today. The ones listed below have been quite effective in many churches and are desirable as starting points for churches who have no witnessing program currently in place. In fact, these have been chosen for examination because of their popularity and the fact that they are helpful in

---

19. Instant evangelism is used by Southard as a descriptive rather than a derogatory adjective. He points out the fact that many evangelistic appeals are characterized by the word *immediacy*. Revivalists often make appeals based on the "lateness of the hour," "before it is too late," and so on.

20. Samuel Southard, *Pastoral Evangelism* (Nashville: Broadman Press, 1962), 24.

communicating the basics in witnessing. They are not being examined as wrong or out-of-date processes.

Many other systems are available and could be examined also. However the reader will catch the direction of the discussion with an examination of just a few current models.

Systems such as the popular Evangelism Explosion (EE) or the Southern Baptist version, Continuing Witness Training (CWT), attempt to elicit a response from a lost person based upon the telling of the gospel using a model outline "plan of salvation" and minimal dialogue. The person being trained is taught how to ask certain questions and is encouraged to listen to the responses.

CWT, for example, teaches the witness to be open to objections, questions, and opportunities for further dialogue during the witnessing encounter. It is important not to overlook the training provided in this method that will keep the witness from making the mistake of ignoring the needs of the listener.

However, a problem arises when emphasis is not placed upon developing the dialogical process during the witnessing encounter and letting it flow toward the presenting of the gospel. The temptation is to get along with the presentation or to listen on a surface level to questions or feedback from the person being talked to. Even though the witness is taught to be sincere in his listening to the person's life situation, some hurry through the process and worry not as much about the listening as about the process that moves toward the presentation of the model plan. Developing a dialogical process based upon listening in witnessing situations is critical to having the lost person understand clearly the plan that is being presented. Do not make the mistake of hurrying through the process while using CWT or EE or any other plan that calls for a model presentation. Learning to enhance dialogue through listening is the kind of atmosphere that a witness should want to create in the encounter.

The real strength of these programs is in their mentoring process, where persons are trained in a model presentation and then taken to the field to witness under the guidance of other trained witnesses. Here the person being trained should observe the way the listening and dialogical process is moving in the witnessing encounter and learn from it. It is therefore important to have someone who understands the importance of listening leading the way. A high level of commitment is required of those who are trained in EE or CWT. Thousands of churches have had enormous success using these systems.

However, some churches find that the process has a few drawbacks. One is the memorization or learning of vast amounts of material for the model presentation of the gospel. The requirements for memorization often limit the participation of many who otherwise would be willing to be a part of the mentoring process that the systems afford.

Another problem has to do with the standardization of the witnessing process itself, which can lead to the discouragement of dialogue if carried too far. Recently, in a conference with forty pastors, I asked how many of them adapted such systems to the context of their church field, and how many used the material exactly as it is taught "off the shelf." Without exception every pastor indicated the need to adapt the process and often to explain the gospel presentation. Not a single one indicated that he advocated the use of the material exactly as it is taught. This seems to be a positive move. CWT even goes so far as to give persons three opportunities to express any questions or concerns that may have been raised during the witnessing process. It may be that the demographics of the area will require a lot of time in dialogue or in explaining what Christians believe. It may be necessary to depart from the outline in order to clarify concepts. This is a valid process.

Some trainers, however, teach people not to vary away from the process or the witnessing outline being used. When people ask questions, they are often dealt with quickly and then the witness is taught to get back on track with his presentation. This is a danger. Ideally these processes teach witnesses to listen carefully and to even restate concerns raised by a lost person before proceeding with the witness encounter to make sure that they have been heard. This is a critical part of training that should not be overlooked. On several occasions they have been overlooked, as we shall see, and the result has led to discouragement with the method.

The approaches that use model presentations have been very successful in many cases. They tend to work best with people who are religiously oriented—that is, persons who understand the flow of the presentation in terms of the religious language used. There are exceptions.

However, in a world of increasing intolerance for sales pitches, many people do not care to listen and will not respond to a memorized approach being thrown at them. They can be quite reluctant to accept any person who comes at them proclaiming anything, whether it be the gospel or an invitation to a ski vacation at a timesharing condo.

A lot of people today are predisposed to disregarding the gospel message. Many lost people have never had a quality or extended conversation with a Christian and do not expect to. Hence, they quickly turn aside if the discussion veers toward religious things. They are quick to form opinions about the gospel with little or no real understanding of what drives most Christians to want to share in the first place.

Evangelism presented exclusively as manipulative proclamation and persuasion easily becomes the victim of much resistance in today's suspicious secular society. If lost and secular persons do listen, it is often without such commitment.

I was in a restaurant with several pastor friends. We were at a round table and the waitress was working hard to keep the lot of us served. We were laughing and having a good time of fellowship. I noticed that the waitress was not very conversational. She was absorbed in her work.

At the end of the meal, the waitress came to present the check to the group. One of the pastors began to talk to her. She was standing there with a tray in one hand on her way to another table. The pastor asked her if she was saved. She said, "No." He presented the plan of salvation and asked her if she would be willing to ask Christ into her heart right then and there. She agreed, and with the waitress standing over the table, the pastors at the table all bowed their heads and the person doing the witnessing led in a prayer that he asked her to repeat.

When the prayer began, I peeked at the waitress and watched her through the whole prayer. She had her head bowed slightly and was repeating the prayer that she was being led to pray. But one thing struck me. While everyone else had heads bowed and eyes closed and were listening to her pray, she was looking up, glancing at her tables and customers while she was repeating the prayer she was being led to pray. I wondered if she would be like so many who claim to be saved. At some point they overhear the gospel, pray a prayer, but may never really receive Christ. Hans Kasdorf is probably right. "A man convinced against his will is of the same opinion still."[21]

The idea of always using a "plan of salvation" or a memorized approach, sometimes called a "canned approach" by those who do not approve of it as a method, should not prevent us from presenting the gospel in other ways. The evangelist should feel the freedom to use other ap-

---

21. Hans Kasdorf, *Christian Conversion in Context* (Scottdale, Pa.: Herald Press, 1980), 58.

proaches, including a dialogical method. But many are highly critical of the dialogical approach for fear that it takes too long or results in a watering down of the urgency often implicit in the more direct approach—that it never gets to the gospel.

Paris Reidhead is so suspicious of always using a plan of salvation that he says, by insisting on a plan of salvation, it may be possible to neglect the person of Jesus Christ Himself. Reidhead finds that many within the church have reduced "so great salvation" to a formula, a plan, a decision to "accept Christ" that has little impact on a person's daily life.[22] Many, Reidhead fears, accept the plan and never get to the place where they understand the message of life transformation that is the basis for the plan's design in the first place.

John McArthur has warned that persons who receive Christ to simply get out from underneath a feeling of guilt, yet with no intention of submitting themselves to the lordship of Christ, have simply convinced themselves that they are saved when in actuality there has never been any evidence of the new birth like the Bible talks about.[23] How else can one explain the numbers of Christians who have doubtless been presented the gospel, accepted it, and yet still lie, cheat, steal, and conduct shady business deals as a matter of course in the conduct of their daily affairs?

Churches across America can attest to membership rolls that contain the names of many who made decisions but who never attend anymore or cannot be located. The open sore in church life today is the large back door that exists in

22. Paris Reidhead, *Getting Evangelicals Saved* (Minneapolis: Bethany House, 1989), statement on the back cover.
23. See *The Gospel According to Jesus* by John McArthur (Grand Rapids: Zondervan, 1988). His book is an excellent examination of the problems encountered when Christians do not take seriously the issue of the lordship of Christ in the process of salvation.

most churches. Many come in the front door, make a decision, and then drop out of sight, possibly never to enter the
church's life again. Spiritual stillbirth is a sad reality among
millions. It seems for these people that the gospel has not
been effectively translated from the pages of the Bible and
into daily life. Obviously, Reidhead and others point to a legitimate concern.

Hans Kasdorf has pointed out that the New Testament
apostles were very successful in translating the ancient concepts for righteous living in the Old Testament from the Hebrew context into the context of the Greek soul and mind.
They put the Old Testament prophecies and promises of a
Savior into the modern dress of the Hellenistic language and
day.[24] As Michael Green has observed, without such a task
of translation the message would have been heard perhaps,
but not assimilated.[25]

Paul the apostle was skillful as a communicator. He
could do exactly what Kasdorf has suggested. And he could
also take a person not familiar with the Hebrew religion and
move them to an understanding of what he had to say. He
used illustrations from the Greek religious culture itself in
Athens and began to dialogue with his listeners about his
faith. More and more, as America continues to move into a
post-Christian era, witnesses will be called upon to dialogue
from Mars Hill.

---

*"The problem comes when we settle on
one single method of presenting the
gospel to the exclusion of all others . . ."*

---

24. Kasdorf, *Christian Conversion,* 58.
25. Michael Green, *Evangelism in the Early Church* (Grand Rapids: Eerdmans,
1975), 115.

Among many today, the assimilation of the gospel has evidently not taken place, even though they have been presented the gospel oftentimes through the vehicle of gospel plans and presentations. It might be well to understand how we came to limit gospel presentations to always using a plan.

The Plan of Salvation—A Caveat

Before I enter this section of the book I want to make it very clear that I believe all evangelism is confrontational in nature. Anytime the gospel is shared with another (and it must be done verbally) and that person has to come face to face with his personal sinfulness before God, confrontation takes place. And it is healthy. It leads to salvation. Even in the most inductive approach one might use to talk to people about Christ, there must come a point at which the other person confronts the claims of Christ and His gospel, the lostness of his life, the need of a Savior, and the need to submit his life under the Lordship of Jesus Christ. Hence, evangelism always involves a verbal witness to the facts and demands of the gospel.

The problem comes when we settle on one single method of presenting the gospel to the exclusion of all others, refine it, and dole it out as a magic formula that will apply to every situation, everywhere, every time. For example, among certain world religions or cult groups a presentation using a memorized plan simply does not work. Bill Gordon tells of a person who had been trained using a memorized approach to the gospel. He had evidently used the approach effectively among many to whom he had witnessed. However, one day he met a New Age person. He began to ask the diagnostic question, "Suppose you were standing before God right now and He were to ask you, 'Why should I let you into My heaven?' What would be your response?" To which the New Age advocate replied, "I have you to know, sir, that I

am God and that I would never ask myself that question!"
The man was speechless. He did not know how to continue
in his gospel presentation. Gordon emphasized in the telling
of the story that he would have been more effective with the
New Age devotee had he sat down and dialogued about spiritual things in general and then moved toward presentation
of the fundamentals of the faith.[26]

In my own experience I know that Bill is right. I have
used every kind of presentation I have ever been taught in my
own personal witnessing. And I will continue to use tracts,
my personal testimony, a marked New Testament, model
outlines and other presentations. But in many cases I have
also quietly sat for hours, sometimes over a period of weeks
and months in careful dialogue with another. We have discussed the gospel over coffee. We have shared together on
the golf course, in his living room and at his office. Then has
come the breakthrough when the person was willing to pray
to receive Jesus as Savior. It was not a quick fix, but a slow
process. *So please understand that this book is not intended
to debunk any method of telling another about Jesus or to
otherwise undermine any process.* Rather, it is intended to
help us clearly see other options and to add at least one more
option, that of listening and dialogue, to the many available
to us. And in adding this option of listening and dialogue, it
is necessary to sometimes look at possible weaknesses and
omissions in other methods.

I am concerned that many of our training methods in
evangelism fall far short of fully equipping others to share
their faith. Often guilt is the primary motivator of persons to
witness. The underlying message is that if they do not attend
a witnessing class, take a course, or present the gospel on a
regular basis with everyone they meet that they are not being

---

26. Interview with Bill Gordon, regional Interfaith Witness director, Home Mission Board, Atlanta, Ga.

faithful as witnesses. Some hold the opinion that persons who witness as a matter of lifestyle are not anxious to present the gospel and that they will do anything they can to avoid presenting the gospel verbally. We must find some common ground between these two approaches. I believe that bringing a strong listening and dialogical process into all our witnessing encounters will add strength to what we are trying to accomplish.

". . . many churches train witnesses but do not provide them any ongoing support through the process."

Assumptions are sometimes made that when a person has gone through a class, passed a test, or demonstrated skills in presenting the gospel, she is certified for witnessing in the real world. But what about those situations where you encounter persons who are not religiously oriented? What if they do not know even the basics about Christianity, the Bible, or faith?

Another significant problem is that many churches train witnesses but do not provide them any ongoing support through the process. Persons who try to share their faith on a regular basis need the support that a group can offer. They need an opportunity to debrief. They need to be able to talk with others about roadblocks they encounter in the witnessing process.

Jim Peterson has provided an excellent model through a video series called *Living Proof,* published by the Christian Businessmen's Committee of Navigators. In this model the witness reports back to an ongoing group, where each member is in process with a lost person. Problems are discussed and hints are given to aid the witness in the ongoing encounter. This debriefing session that can meet from time to time or on a regular basis to follow up on the progress of witnessing encounters is an element that is missing from most training programs offered in local churches. Personal witnessing classes and programs take an enormous amount of time to do well. Commitment must be made to the whole process if many are going to stick to their training over the long haul. Research has shown that many churches who complete one cycle of training in personal witnessing often fail to get the second cycle off the ground. Without ongoing supervision and follow-up in the process, little is accomplished in reality.

Today is Saturday. I played golf this morning. It was one of those few weekends where I had a Saturday off from conference leading or traveling, so it was a nice change. In my golf bag I have several clubs. Golfers use a variety of clubs in their bag, depending on where the ball lies, how far it is from the hole, and how strong the golfer's swing is. It would be foolish to try to use a putter on every stroke from the tee to the green. Likewise, to use a sand wedge when the putter is called for would be a disaster for the shot and for the green.

Yet many times what we advocate in evangelism is only one method of witnessing. When preachers and conference leaders talk about sharing the faith, one image pops into the minds of most people. It is sharing one-on-one with a stranger some gospel presentation or tract on the Tuesday or Thursday night visitation. This was demonstrated in a survey of more than a thousand pastors as they were asked to define evangelism.[27]

Recently a pastor friend of mine told me a story that illustrated the point above very clearly. He was sitting at home

---

27. Ronald W. Johnson, "An Evaluation of the Home Mission Board Programs of Evangelism in Local Churches." unpublished D. Min. thesis, The Southern Baptist Theological Seminary, 1988.

one evening, relaxing after a hard day. The doorbell rang. He opened the door and there stood a fellow pastor and two other persons he did not recognize.

He greeted the pastor and asked why they had come to his house.

"Well, we were in the neighborhood and we prayed and God seemed to be directing us to witness to the people in this house." one of the laypersons said.

"That's interesting," said my pastor friend. "I'm sure that I could use your prayers, because my wife and I have been sort of strung out and busy during the last week or so with all that is going on in our church." And so the group prayed together.

"By the way," the other pastor commented, "I heard you just completed your doctorate. What field did you finish in?" he asked.

My friend responded, "I did my doctorate in evangelism."

To which the other pastor smiled and beamed, "Then I guess you like going house to house and presenting the plan of salvation and using (he named a certain witnessing process)."

"Well, I actually do not use that approach." my friend said.

The laypersons with the pastor gasped. "Why not?" one asked.

He carefully explained that some people in their community were not religiously oriented. These people did not understand much of what we as religiously oriented persons take for granted, such as the ease with which we use religious language or our understanding of the importance of prayer, and that many secular persons do not even know simple Scripture passages, let alone the complex tenets of salvation. "Our church has decided to carry the gospel to these kinds of people. We are in the jails, in soup kitchens, in hospitals, on the streets, and in the places where people who never come to church often hang out. We've decided to approach these people more inductively. We spend time with them and talk with them over enough of a time period so that we can get across what becoming a Christian is all about," my friend shared.

"But when do you present them the plan of salvation?" one of the laypersons asked. The pastor did not comment.

"We do it all along in the process of dialoguing and sharing in their life experiences," he said.

"But don't you show them that the Bible is the Word of God and that it says they must be saved?" another asked.

"These people don't know the Bible. Nor do many of them trust it. They are secular. They do not have a religious orientation to life like you do," my pastor friend said.

The conversation went on for some time with the three at the door trying to make a case for approaching every person the same way in presenting the gospel plan of salvation. My pastor friend tried to show how his church was trying to meet people in their life situation, and to move them to a place where they could attach some meaning and appreciation to the gospel itself. Needless to say, an impasse was reached. The group turned away from my friend and left, convinced that he was not really a witness after all.

What happens when religiously oriented persons assume that nonreligiously oriented persons understand the basic tenets of Christianity and have some affinity for the things of God? The fact is, they often do not. They are not necessarily hostile to the things of God. Rather, religion for them is irrelevant. Active faith in God is not a part of their life's agenda. We are living in a post-Christian culture. It is one that no longer leans toward the things of God, but away from the things of God. For the secular evangelism becomes what Williman calls a "gracious, unmanageable, merry, by-product of the intrusion of God."[28] Most Christians have been sheltered from this reality, and it is quite possible that many do not realize that it is reality. The only friends many of us have are other Christians. We are not inviting secular persons over to our homes for backyard cookouts and going on trips together with them. Yet we present the gospel assuming that everyone is like the people we deal with in our churches and those from our Sunday School classes who visit our house on the weekends. Listen to a typical gospel presentation. You will find out that it often takes a lot for granted, is often unclear and sounds very mechanical to non-religiously oriented persons. Even the phrases we use, "accept Jesus Christ as personal Savior," "ask Jesus into your heart," "invite Christ into your life," or "make a decision" are terms that are foreign to many people.[29]

I heard a preacher tell a story about a little boy. His childhood friend invited him to go to church with him. The young lad had never been to church before in his life. His father was an alcoholic and his mother cared little about spiritual things. In the Sunday School class the teacher bowed his head and began to pray. He ended his prayer with the usual ending that most Christians are taught to pray, "in the name of Jesus Christ, Amen."

The little boy became upset and asked the teacher, "Why did you use those swear words in your prayer?" The Sunday School teacher was surprised at the question and asked the young boy what he meant, all the while insisting that he had used no swear words in his prayer. "Oh yes you did," the young boy said. "My father also uses those words when he swears," he said. "What words?" asked the teacher. "You know . . . Jesus Christ," the boy said. The only time this young lad had ever heard about Jesus was in the context of swearing. Such is the day and time we are living in.

---

28. William Williman, *The Intrusive Word* (Grand Rapids: Eerdmans, 1994), 4.
29. John F. McArthur, Jr., *The Gospel According to Jesus* (Grand Rapids: Zondervan, 1988), 21.

Many scholars insist that we are living in a post-Christian era. In fact, when you meet the average person on the street in America today you can no longer pre-suppose that he has a religious orientation to life, particularly a Judeo-Christian orientation. And you can no longer pre-suppose that he will understand what you are saying when you present the gospel. McArthur argues that you may be so accustomed to hearing those phrases (religious words used when presenting the gospel) that it will surprise you to learn none of them is based on biblical terminology.[30] But these terms are often tossed around in many presentations of the plan of salvation. And the plan of salvation has become almost the only vehicle for sharing the gospel in the minds of Christians. This model then, loaded with words that we take for granted as Christians, may be as foreign to the lost, non-religiously oriented person as most software programming jargon is to the layperson trying to use his lap-top.

THE PLAN OF SALVATION

The "plan of salvation" means different things to different people. Some Christians think immediately of the Roman Road (presenting the gospel using various texts from the book of Romans), or tracts such as the *Four Spiritual Laws* from Campus Crusade, or the *Eternal Life* tract from Southern Baptists. Among other groups in history, THE PLAN, had many meanings. Samuel Southard gives an excellent summary in his book, *Pastoral Evangelism*.[31]

The Disciples of the early nineteenth century understood "the plan" to mean that baptism preceded remission of sins and the gift of the Holy Spirit.[32] Calvinism saw the plan

---

30. Ibid.
31. Southard, *Pastoral Evangelism*.
32. Jesse R. Kellems, *Alexander Campbell and the Disciples* (New York: Richard R. Smith, Inc., 1930), 1930.

as synonymous with the "order of decrees" or the process by which God determined the redemption of the world.[33] In 1887, James Walker published a book on the *Philosophy of the Plan of Salvation* and focused upon personal salvation. Spurgeon preached *Twelve Sermons on the Plan of Salvation* (C. H. Spurgeon, 1892).[34] "The 'plan of salvation' was a phrase that might be heard in many churches of the late nineteenth and early twentieth centuries."[35]

> *"Neither Moody nor Spurgeon advised a rigid 'plan' in their talks to Christians who desired to witness to others."*

However, as Southard points out, in the evangelism of the previous generations, "this phrase did not indicate a step-by-step, rigid system of conversion."[36] These preachers and writers were thinking in a holistic manner about salvation, not systematically. Even Jonathan Edwards (1746) stated that there was no definite order in the process by which a man develops the "new sense" of God.[37] Southard points out that a hundred years later Charles Finney presented a variety of methods by which God's grace would be extended toward sinners.

Neither Moody nor Spurgeon advised a rigid "plan" in their talks to Christians who desired to witness to others. It is

---

33. Benjamin Warfield, *The Plan of Salvation* (Grand Rapids: Wm. B. Eerdmans Publishing Company, 1942), 13, 101.
34. Southard, 29.
35. Ibid., 24.
36. Ibid., 29.
37. Ibid.

interesting that these two men are often held up as models in evangelism, yet they advocated no rigid, single presentation. Moody stood by his conviction that "God never repeats himself; he does not approach any two people the same way." He went on to say, "What I want first to call your attention to, if you are going to be successful in winning souls to Christ, is the need for discrimination in finding out people's differences."[38]

When specific steps were suggested, as Southard points out, they were explained in R. A. Torrey's *How to Work for Christ*. Torrey sought to help people who realized their need for salvation and who already *wanted* to be saved.

Mullins' classic *The Christian Religion in Its Doctrinal Expression* affirmed the instantaneous work of God in salvation but rejected a swift, stereotyped, superficial assurance of salvation to the inquirer.[39] Southard points out that the twentieth century saw a diminishing of flexible approaches to soul-winning. This focus on more structural approaches seems to be in keeping with a move in the twentieth century to structure most of society more tightly. It can be seen in education, science, philosophy, and other disciplines. "By the 1920s the 'plan of salvation' was systematized and applied to personal witnessing."[40] A popular example was Austin Crouch's *Plan of Salvation* (1924). Conversion was reduced to a five-step outline:

1. Show the one with whom you are dealing that he is a sinner and therefore lost.

2. Show the one with whom you are dealing that he cannot save himself.

---

38. Ibid., 30. See also Dwight L. Moody, *Great Joy* (New York: E. B. Treat & Co., 1877),277.
39. Southard, *Pastoral Evangelism,* 30.
40. Ibid., 31.

3. Show the one with whom you are dealing that Christ can save him.

4. Show the one with whom you are dealing that Christ will save him on two conditions (repentance and faith).

5. Show the one with whom you are dealing the duty of a believer in Christ. (It is the duty of Christians to serve Christ: the faithful servant will be rewarded when the Master comes; the disobedient servant will be chastised in this life).[41]

Crouch's plan was a formula, a fairly rigid approach to reaching people with the gospel. It did not allow for differences in people as Moody had suggested.

Crouch was out of step with men like Edwards, Finney, Moody, Spurgeon, and E. Y. Mullins. "Yet the twentieth-century plan has been widely adopted by many evangelical groups."[42] Today the emphasis in many soul-winning encounters and campaigns is exclusively the presentation of the *plan of salvation.*

Compare, for example, the outline of "A Presentation of the Gospel" in the popular course, *Evangelism Explosion.*

I.   The Introduction

    A. Their secular life

    B. Their church background

    C. Our church

    D. Testimony: personal or church

    E. Two Questions:

        1. Have you come to a place in your spiritual life where you know for certain that if you were to die today you would go to heaven?

---

41. Ibid.
42. Ibid., 32.

2. Suppose that you were to die tonight and stand before God and He were to say to you, "Why should I let you into My heaven?" What would you say?

II. The Gospel

  A. Grace

    1. Heaven is a free gift

    2. It is not earned or deserved

  B. Man

    1. Is a sinner

    2. Cannot save himself

  C. God

    1. Is merciful—therefore doesn't want to punish us

    2. Is just—therefore must punish sin

  D. Christ

    1. Who He is—the infinite God-man

    2. What He did—He paid for our sins and purchased a place in heaven for us which He offers as a gift which may be received by . . .

  E. Faith

    1. What it is not—mere intellectual assent nor temporal faith

    2. What it is—"not" trusting in Jesus Christ alone for our salvation"

III. The Commitment

  A. The qualifying question

  B. The commitment question

  C. The clarification of commitment

  D. The prayer of commitment

  E. The assurance of salvation[43]

Notice the construct of this presentation. It is very systematic, deductive and juridical. It makes perfect sense to the Anglo-American mind with an evangelical orientation. But what happens when this process is used with some ethnic groups?

Southern Baptists have published millions of the *Eternal Life* tract. This tract goes along with the model presentation used in the popular CWT training process. It begins, as does Evangelism Explosion, with the diagnostic questions:

1. Have you come to a place in your spiritual life where you know for certain that if you were to die today you would go to heaven?

2. Suppose that you were to die tonight and stand before God and He were to say to you, "Why should I let you into My heaven?" What would you say?

The tract goes on to present the gospel in a logical manner. "God Has a Plan For Your Life." But how does it work among some ethnic groups?

A friend of mine told me that he was involved in trying to train Chinese pastors in the approach. There were about fifty pastors present in the training session. The tract was being demonstrated. The pastors listened attentively. The instructor told the pastors that they would find copies of the tract in Chinese on their pews. They were instructed to pick up the tract and to turn to another person and practice the use of the tract as had been demonstrated. The tract had been translated directly from the English to the Chinese.

Nothing happened. The pastors continued to sit very rigidly in the pews and to smile at their leader. He instructed them once again. Nothing happened. The instructor knew he was in trouble. So he dismissed the class for a break. He called his long-time Chinese friend to his side to find out

---

43. James Kennedy, *Evangelism Explosion* (Wheaton: Tyndale House, 1972), 21.

why the session had gone so poorly. He was surprised to hear the answer. "In our culture we do not use that method for witnessing," he told the American.

"In our culture we tell stories. The pastors did not want to be rude and question your authority, so they just sat still." he continued. "They like you, they just do not like your methods."

It might be obvious that a model presentation or rigid system might not work among certain ethnic groups, but the fact is that in today's culture, it is also suspect among many Anglo-Americans. People still prefer stories told in an interesting way over most any other kind of communication. The Master Teacher told stories and it worked well for Him.

Compare the popular *Four Spiritual Laws* used by Campus Crusade.[44]

▲ Law One "God Loves You and Offers a Wonderful Plan for Your Life."

▲ Law Two "Man Is Sinful and Separated from God. Thus HeCannot Know and Experience God's Love and Plan for His Life."

▲ Law Three "Jesus Christ IS God's Only Provision for Man's Sin. Through Him You Can Know and Experience God's Love and Plan For Your Life.

▲ Law Four "We Must Individually Receive Jesus Christ as Savior And Lord; Then We Can Know and Experience God's Love and Plan for Our Lives."

Again, what you will notice is a systematized presentation, with a rather linear movement toward resolution. The discussion begins with God, moves to His plan, man's separation from God, God's provision for man's sin, and man's

---

44. Bill Bright, *Have You Heard of the Four Spiritual Laws?* (Arrowhead Springs, San Bernardino: Campus Crusade for Christ International).

response. While both presentations are logical, sensible, and easy to utilize, they make the assumption that the person listening is quite capable of decoding linear thought, and systematic structure, and following logical progression. Each person who goes through Evangelism Explosion (or Continuing Witness Training, the Southern Baptist version) learns the above outline or some variation of it. While the outline does allow some flexibility if the individual chooses—that is, she may add to the content or seek to explain it in her own words, the process is fairly rigid by design. This is evident because the requirements of these versions, especially CWT, require that she be tested in her ability to recite the memorized model or plan before being certified as a witness.

"Certainly Christians need to employ every tool possible to share effectively their faith."

In many churches and denominational programs today, evangelism has been limited to the presentation of this kind of plan. Presenting the gospel is synonymous with presenting the plan. A large number of church leaders train members using highly structured approaches to the lost. Some might criticize an approach that does not elevate the importance of a plan. They might say that without a plan there is no direction or they'd rather know a plan of salvation and have something to say than to not be properly equipped to share the faith. There is something to this argument.

Some people will use the lack of a plan as an excuse for not sharing. Some will likewise criticize the use of a plan as an excuse for not sharing the gospel. *Those who want to find an excuse for not sharing the faith will quickly find one.*

However, what is important to note here in the discussion of
the concept of a plan of salvation is that it should not be
thought of as the *only* tool to use in sharing the faith. To
many Christians the plan of salvation is so much a part of our
language and religious culture that it has been communicated
as the one and only tool for sharing the gospel. But witnessing can take many forms of expression. Certainly Christians
need to employ every tool possible to share effectively their
faith. Taking into consideration the context of every situation and every person's unique need can only bring strength
to the witness encounter.

THE NEED FOR DIALOGUE

George Hunter calls for an approach to evangelism that
is more dialogical. He believes that secular people are essentially ignorant of basic Christianity and need to be engaged
in dialogue if they are going to really listen to or understand
the gospel. And it is necessary because the world has
changed so much. No longer can we rely on the fact that people understand basic Christian doctrine. As Lord Donald
Soper says, "to ignore the manifold differences of outlook
and circumstance which have crowded in on modern people
is as fatal for evangelism as it is for politics and economics.
The communicator, if he or she is to be heard, must begin
with the listener where the listener is, and not where the
evangelist thinks he or she ought to be."[45] Many times Christians have been answering questions that the secular persons
have not been asking, scratching where people were not itch-
ing.

---

45. George Hunter, *How to Reach Secular People* (Nashville: Abingdon, 1992),
11–12. See also Kenneth W. Inskeep, "A Short History of Church Growth Research," in *Church and Denominational Growth*, ed. by David A. Roozen and C.
Kirk Hathaway (Nashville: Abingdon, 1993), 144–45.

According to Hunter, "the church has relied on author-
itative preaching to reach the unchurched masses, but most
secular people experience such preaching as authoritarian
preaching. It turns them off, or they are merely amused by
the 'great pulpit oratory' that many church people still
love."[46] Recently in a revival I was preaching the pastor told
me to "turn up the wick," that his people loved good preaching. What he meant was they loved the oratory!

> *". . . what we do on Sunday is to preach*
> *messages that the intended audience*
> *never hears."*

I have attended thousands of hours of church worship
services during my life. Preaching has been a special part of
those services. I have been challenged and I have been
touched by many of the messages that I have heard through
the years. There have been a few times in my own preaching
when I have been strangely warmed by the Spirit of God.

But I have also reflected over much of the preaching I
have heard through the years. And I have felt that what we
do on Sunday is to preach messages that the intended audience never hears. I am reminded of the setting of Pentecost
when Peter preached. There were large numbers of lost people there to hear him. He preached to secular people, idola-
ters, and religious people such as the Pharisees in the crowd.
The gospel took hold of many in that setting. In the history
of our own country the frontier was often touched with the
gospel message as lost people willingly came to camp meetings, brush arbors, or to frontier revival meetings. But today,
most preaching is being done within churches, where large
numbers of lost and secular people do not attend by choice.
I was visiting relatives a few weeks back and went with them

---

46. Ibid., 57.

to church. It was a small church, as most Southern Baptist churches are. I knew its history very well. The pastor lacked any formal Bible training. There were about fifty people present. I listened to the message he preached with great interest.

His message was very evangelistic. Though he lacked formal training, he delivered the message with passion and with some oratorical skill. But as I looked around the congregation more than 90 percent of them were lifelong members of that church. They were older people who had lived in the community for years. Those who were not yet Christians or members of the church were the few young children who were there. Nobody in the service could be characterized as part of the 170 million lost people that the Southern Baptist Convention's Home Mission Board describes as the pagan pool. The young children there more than likely would eventually join the church through a profession of faith.

The point is that this church is not the exception. The preacher was preaching a passionate evangelistic message that lost persons needed to hear, but there were few there to hear him. At least none that we would characterize as part of that number with little or no religious orientation to life.

There is a sadness that takes hold of me when I am asked to preach a revival and night after night there are no lost persons in the crowd. Sometimes I can almost predict if there will be anyone there who is lost by observing how much preparation has gone into the revival meeting. Some churches plan well. They visit, invite the lost, go into the community durng the day, and do other things to attract lost persons. But even then, many of the lost who come as a result of the church's efforts are people who have an interest in religious things compared to the secular world. It has been a long, long time since I saw a person converted in a church service who is distinctly from a non-religious orientation to life. How will the message of Jesus Christ ever get to the lost world where the prostitutes, drug addicts, thieves, homosexuals, and agnostics live if we continue to preach it only to those who have already heard?

Preaching will always have a place in the process of proclamation of the gospel, especially among church people. But it is time to change the location and kind of preaching we do. The preached message can no longer be delivered exclusively within the walls of churches. It has to get into the bloodstream of society's everyday life. And the kind of preaching that needs to be done must take on a completely different form from Sunday preaching services.

When the secular lost person of today perceives that we who want to be evangelists have invaded the marketplace, the sports arena, or her home and are preaching at her the way we preach in our churches, instead of conversing with her about the faith, the chances are very remote that much evangelism is going to take place.

Christianity's image has suffered at the hands of TV preachers, crusaders, stereotypes, and flim-flam artists. The unfortunate thing is that the power of the media to impact and influence public opinion has fallen into the hands of many who are hostile toward Christianity. Sitcoms, news programs, and commentaries have taken the negatives and built them into jokes, news stories, and sensationalism. This approach might sell air-time, but it sure hurts the local church's agenda. The image of Christians, the pastor, and those who are sincere witnesses has been dealt a knock-out punch in the last few years. We simply must recover, get back into the ring, and convince a secular world that we really are genuine. The image problem cannot be overlooked. Churches are going to have to work even harder to demonstrate that they care. They will be in the mode of proving their significance to a lot of people as we become more and more a secular country.

Telling the gospel to the secular person will require our best listening skills. Certainly the skill of dialogue with the lost will have to be enhanced in whatever method we choose. And a major part of that dialogue will require sensitive, caring, heart-felt listening.

THINGS TO THINK ABOUT

1. EXPLORE THE CONCEPTS.

Review the sounds that bothered you this day. Think of the sounds you missed hearing today. What level are you listening on? How much do you ignore? Are you a talker or a listener? What distractions do you need to get rid of so that you will be a better listener?

2. SEARCH THE SCRIPTURES.

Look in a concordance and find all the Scriptures you can that deal with listening. Study them in context for further insight. Discuss them in a small group or with a friend.

3. DISCUSS THE PRINCIPLES.

How were you trained to witness? Have you always used a plan? If so, what kind of plan? Have you ever felt that the plan limited your discussion? Enhanced your discussion? How? In what specific ways? If you had never heard of a plan of salvation, how would you witness to a lost person? How important is dialogue in your own personal witnessing approach? How much do you dialogue?

4. ACT ON WHAT YOU HAVE LEARNED.

Talk to other Christians about how they witness. Find someone this week with whom you can discuss the method of witnessing that you both have always used. Talk together about the strengths and the weaknesses in using a dialogical method rather than a plan in every situation. If you used dialogue in a witnessing situation, how would you guide the person toward knowing Christ? Discuss some ways.

Chapter 3

LISTENING WITH BOTH EARS

"Speak, Lord, for your servant is listening."

1 Samuel 3:9

Modern people lack silence. So says the late Paul Tournier, M.D., author and popular speaker. In his book, *A Listening Ear, Reflections on Christian Caring*, Tournier tells us that people no longer live their lives, but are instead dragged along by events.[1] That certainly seems to be the case in most of the lives I have noticed.

---

1. Paul Tournier, *A Listening Ear, Reflections on Christian Caring* (Minneapolis: Augsburg Publishing House, 1984), 12.

People run from event to event, from place to place, and we are so busy we have little time for anything but the activity of running from appointment to appointment; and all this occurs in a day when we are supposed to have more leisure time available to us than ever before! Stress is now one of the major killers of Americans. Calendar sales are at an all time high as people segment and otherwise try to organize their busy lives.

Tournier reasoned that many of his patients came to see him "to find a quiet, peaceful person who knows how to listen and who isn't thinking all the time about what he has to do next."[2] His peaceful demeanor came, no doubt, from his experience of practicing quietness and meditation for over fifty years.

But most of us have no idea how to be quiet. We have forgotten to do as the psalmist tells us, to "be still and know" that He is God (Ps. 46:10). I would imagine that the psalmist is trying to tell us to be like God in the process of listening.

THE LISTENING GOD

Have you ever thought how much God has to listen to? He listens to our prayers and thoughts toward Him. The remarkable thing is that, with all the listening that God must do, He does it on an individual basis. We can learn a lesson here.

Listening to people is a very individualized process. It focuses for the moment on the person, her hopes, dreams, fears, aspirations and goals. Jesus showed us how to listen like that. As Norman Wakefield notes about Jesus, He took time to listen,

God's compassionate, listening heart is seen clearly in Jesus Christ. During His earthly visit He

---

2. Ibid.

*attracted multitudes, not merely by what He said,
but equally by His willingness to listen to the individual's distressing circumstances. After hearing
the full message, He would respond with the appropriate word or touch. Jesus listens.[3]*

It can truthfully be said that if our lives are noisy, so full
of our own agenda of activities and events, the chances are
remote that we will ever be effective Jesus-style listeners.

How critical it is for us to learn the truth of quietness.
Someone has said that silence is golden. Certainly we must
learn to discipline ourselves to apply that silence, especially
if we are going to be caring tellers of the good news. Wayne
Oates has said that the reality of silence is no mere "gimmick" for manipulating people. For it to be meaningful, a listening silence must transcend the dreary fate of being a
"technique" of pastoral counseling.[4] We need to learn to listen genuinely with both ears, to wait before God. How else
will you know what to say to a lost person?

"Something happens when we listen to others."

Something happens when we listen to others. As Tournier said, when we so listen to a person, he has felt understood.
When we listen to him, we help him to live and to face even
the most difficult of situations. We give him confidence.[5]
After all, isn't that what Jesus did? Didn't He give people
confidence to believe on Him? I tend to think one of Jesus'

3. Norman Wakefield, *Listening: A Christian's Guide to Loving Relationships*
(Waco: Word Books, 1981), 15.
4. Wayne Oates, *The Presence of God in Pastoral Counseling* (Dallas: Word
Publishing, 1986), 70.
5. Joyce Huggett, *Listening to Others* (Downers Grove: InterVarsity Press,
1988), 88.

most formidable challenges was to develop the confidence of
His rag-tag group so that they would come to realize that
they would do greater works than He ever did. Being a listener to people is a skill that has to be developed. To develop
that skill and an understanding of it will require an examination of the mechanics of listening.

HOW WE LISTEN

The whole study into how we listen is a recent field of
research. About 90 percent of the listening research has been
done only since the 1950s. While many of us were getting
polio vaccines as children, the researchers were just beginning to think about and understand more fully how we listen.
Nevertheless, it is a fascinating process, this listening—and
it is complex.

Have you ever heard the old conundrum, "If a tree falls
in the forest, and no one is around to hear it fall, will a sound
be made?" Well, as far as human beings go, if they are not
present, it is really a moot point. If no one is there to hear it,
the sound will be of no effect, even though the vibrations of
the air waves have been at full force. That is because listening involves a hearer and hearers attach meaning to the
event. Indeed, the whole process of listening requires a hearer who can assign meaning to his experiences.

Listening starts with sound, whether generated by a
falling tree or a politician giving an impassioned speech. The
tree and the politician cause a physical disturbance to occur
in the air waves that hit our ear drums. And hearing begins
for us.

Although the listener is unaware of it, he does not receive words or noise, but rather sound waves. And these
sound waves come bit by bit. Some sound waves are short
and others are long. If someone says "Go," the sound is
shorter than if someone tells you to "Come here." The gath-

ering of sounds and their impact upon the mind are translated in unconscious ways for us. Stanford Taylor has explained that, during the third of a second it takes to hear a syllable, or during the several seconds it takes to listen to an idea, many factors affect the translation of sound into meaning.[6] We scarcely notice the process, but it is certainly correct to understand listening as a process, for at least three steps are involved.[7]

HOW WE HEAR

The first step is the **hearing**. Hearing is the process by which sound waves are received and modified by the ear. There is a mechanical aspect to the way the eardrum works to convert the sound waves impacting the soft tissue of the drum into a stimulus upon the nerves. Most any human anatomy book can be consulted if the reader wishes to see how the tiny bones in the ear function. It is beyond the purpose of this book to give a comprehensive anatomy of the human body's hearing process. Rather, this brief overview will give the reader a general working knowledge of the process. Further study can be found in the sources listed in the footnotes.

EFFICIENCY

Once the sound enters the ear of the listener, the efficiency of the hearing is due to several factors. Everything from physical abnormalities to background noise can affect the hearing process.

6. Stanford Taylor, *Listening* (Washington, D.C.: National Education Association of the United States, 1964).
7. This material is gleaned from Stanford Taylor's booklet that attempted to help teachers understand something about the process of listening. I have tried to summarize Taylor's explanation. This is in no way a complete or technical explanation. For such the will need to consult other sources.

"Human speech comprises frequencies ranging from 125 to 8,000 cycles per second. . . . Within this range, the frequencies between 1,000 and 2,500 c.p.s. furnish the majority of word cues and as such are judged to be most critical. Frequencies above 2,500 c.p.s. contribute to the fineness with which we hear such sounds as b,d,f,g,s,t,v,sh,th, and zh. The intensity, or loudness level, found in everyday speech will range typically from 55 decibels (faint speech) to 85 decibels (loud conversation)."[8]

Some people cannot hear certain ranges and have hearing loss. Stanford Taylor explains, "A person is said to have a hearing loss when he requires more than the normal amount of volume in order to hear sounds of certain frequencies."[9] Students in school are often tested to examine the range of frequencies they can hear and the volume needed to achieve that hearing. "Most important is the detection of those losses in the frequencies above 1,000 c.p.s., since these frequencies are the most critical to the intelligibility of speech."[10]

The cartoons of old men cupping their ear to hear or using an ear horn are no laughing matter when it comes to children who cannot hear the teacher or, for that matter, one who sits in a church pew catching every other word being spoken from the pulpit. This point was demonstrated to me most vividly in a church where I served as interim pastor. The church was rather large and had an auditorium that was narrow but deep. The sound system was primitive. Those sitting in the front were blasted by the two speakers on the front wall and the people in the back could barely hear. I noticed that two rows of pews about three-fourths of the way back were seldom used. I found out why. The way the sound bounced off the concrete walls as it moved toward the back of the audito-

---

8. Taylor, *Listening*, 7.
9. Ibid.
10. Ibid.

rium created a dead spot. Anyone who sat there had a very difficult time making sense out of anything that was said. It dawned on me that if a lost visitor wandered into the church and sat there, he would not know what was being said. He would be distracted so much by the poor sound quality that the gospel message could not get through.

I brought the matter up to the church. After months of negotiation, the church finally decided to spend the money needed to install a first-class system. I do not know if there was a direct correlation or not, but prior to the installation of the system hardly anyone responded at the time of invitation. After the installation and over the period of a year after it was installed more than forty people came to know Christ as Savior! Could it be that finally they could hear the message plainly?

DANGERS TO HEARING

There are certainly dangers involved in hearing. I have a friend who is a jet airplane mechanic. He will tell you that he has lost some of his hearing due to working around jet aircraft year after year. The high pitch of the jet engines has caused him to lose that frequency range in his hearing. Some teens have measurable hearing loss because of years of listening to high intensity music with personal stereo headphone CD players or radios. Doctors are now warning parents of this problem. Other dangers include physical damage due to disease, injury, and neglect.

MASKING

Another problem with hearing comes from masking. Adjacent sounds that compete with human speech can cover the words we wish to hear. Sounds of the same frequency can actually alter one another. Have you ever been listening to a disc on the CD player, relaxing in your easy chair, enjoying the rhythm and tune of a favorite song, only to have the mood broken when someone comes into the room and turns on the television, perhaps at loud volume, and there is a commercial on the air with music blaring? The two sources of music cannot compete with one another. They both lose. There has been a clash of frequencies. They have altered one another. They are as violent to your ear as red dots on a green background are to your eyes. It is confusing to the mind to try to listen to two equally important sounds at the same time. Fatigue can result and both sounds will lose.

Usually, as noise increases, retention of intended content is decreased rather dramatically. If you have ever had the experience of trying to talk to someone in a crowded, noisy restaurant or at a basketball game, you know the futility of the effort. You have to work at keeping your line of thought intact.

In a recent witnessing encounter, one person reported that he never could get the gospel shared because of the young children in the room who were arguing over a toy, the television set with its blaring ads and the teenager's stereo in the next room also competing for the attention of the person who was trying to listen to the evangelist. The witness could barely focus on what he was saying to the lost person because of the adjacent sounds. Not only did it make him nervous in the gospel presentation, but he felt it caused the other person to be unable to focus his attention also.

Masking can be fatal. A friend of mine lost his life because of this characteristic related to hearing. He was listening to his car radio at near full volume and never heard the whistle of a train as he crossed in front of it. The rock music covered up the warnings of the train's whistle. What a terrible waste of life that was, and it was because one eternally unimportant sound (a rock and roll song) covered up the most important sound of all at the time, the train's whistle, the sound that could have saved his life.

AUDITORY FATIGUE

Auditory fatigue is another factor that limits hearing. When we are exposed to sounds of constant frequency, they can have the effect of reducing our ability to hear those frequencies a moment or two later. A monotone or droning voice is not only boring to listen to, but it can cause us to grow tired and to tune out that frequency. Perhaps that is why many people sleep in church! The preacher may be talking in a tone that causes his audience to be unable to focus. And when a sound far outside that set of frequencies occurs, such as when a door slams or a baby suddenly screams, the congregation can actually get a start from it. Have you ever seen that happen and then watched people jump?

I will never forget Miss Lizzie. She was the last of the old time shouters. Our church was a downtown, blue-collar church in the fifties and sixties when Miss Lizzie, then an elderly lady, attended. She loved her Lord, and though her health kept her from coming to church very often, when she did we were all glad to see her. Once in a while, Miss Lizzie would become overwhelmed with her sense of the Spirit of God in the worship service and she would begin to weep softly. Then she would weep louder, until at last she could hold her emotion no longer and she would shout. When she began to shout, people would wake up. Children would stare. But almost every time, sinners would hear from God and people were saved. Her shouts broke the routine of worship and caused people to sit up and listen, some maybe for the first time.

It was possible to observe people physically reacting with sudden surprise or fright when a new sound, such as Miss Lizzie's shouting, occurred. The sudden change in frequency caused them to react in physical ways. Heads turned. They shifted in their seats and the whole dynamic of the worship event changed.

Sound Sequences

A second step is **listening**. This is the whole process of being aware of sound sequences. When one listens to a speech, for example, the ear receives the sound waves, they are translated into stimuli, and the mind begins processing the whole activity. The person's mind identifies the component sounds and then recognizes the familiar sound sequences as known words.

This is done by the avenues of auditory analysis (deciphering words), mental reorganization (arrangement of ideas), and/or association of meaning—that is, connecting the stimuli with an image, feeling or response.[11]

Not too long ago, I heard a song on the radio that I had not heard since my teenage years. When the song came on, every sensory response connected with where I often heard the song came into play. For an instant I was transported back to Friday nights at our favorite teenage hangout, the town bowling alley. I could smell the chiliburgers and almost taste the french fries. And I could hear the bowling balls hitting the pins while the song played on the juke box. I had a physical response that carried me back to my teen years, all because I heard a series of sounds organized as music. When I heard the sounds, my mind gave them meaning, and the meaning was a pleasurable memory for me. When others hear the gospel, remember that the meaning of the gospel is centered in who they, the receiver, are, not the sender.

Factors in Listening

Several factors influence our listening. Attention and concentration are certainly among the first of the factors.

Taylor says that attention may be thought of as the directing of awareness; concentration, as a sustaining of attention.[12]

---

11. Taylor, *Listening,* 6.
12. Ibid., 10.

All of us know the frustration of trying to talk to someone who is not listening. We can speak all we wish, but if the person is not willing to commit to the process and to give us total attention and concentration, the message, regardless of its importance, will go unheeded.

According to Taylor, attention and concentration depend also upon the mental and physical condition of the person who is listening. Surely none of us would be so naive as to think that we could ask someone to listen to the gospel before meeting the needs of a person who is hungry or very tired, for example. We must be aware that people are not always ready to listen just because we are ready to speak. This is one problem with a monological presentation. It often does not allow us to determine whether or not the person is ready to listen.

Our message has to lend itself to being received. "The content must be such that it can be 'taken in stride,' for if the message is too difficult in relation to the listener's ability to assimilate or manipulate ideas, his attention may wane, or he may take refuge in selective listening to escape from what has been referred to as 'information input overload.' On the other hand, the content must be challenging, for if the message is too simple, the listener will soon find relief by taking mental excursions."[13]

When we share the gospel, we must put it into the kind of language that allows people to catch hold of it, to form mental images of it, and to experience a warm response to it. Jesus spoke in parables. Why? Precisely because it allowed people to form mental images: to hear, taste, feel, go back in time, remember, and savor the experience. Assuming that everyone understands our language and the context out of which we share the gospel is to ignore the basic principle that

---

13. Ibid.

people bring a variety of experiences to the witnessing situation.

We may, for example, use churchy language with someone who has had no background in church. We may use middle-class illustrations to help explain what we mean, but we may frustrate the poor because the images connected with our message may be what poor people can only dream of and never hope to attain. Recently, I was in another country where this was dramatically demonstrated to me. The poverty of the country made it impossible for a person living there to conceive of a place like America where food was plentiful, where the stores have dozens of items on the shelves, and where people can afford to live in single-family dwellings. America has been rich for so long that it is almost impossible for us to conceive of the level which some live on in this world. It is always easy for us to define others in terms of our own experience.

Mental Reorganization

Another factor in listening has to do with a process called, mental reorganization. In this process the listener employs a system that will aid retention.[14] For example, when a person calls directory assistance at the telephone company and is given a telephone number to remember, he is likely to repeat the number over and over again even in the process of seeking to dial it. Saying the number in a kind of chant helps the mind to remember the sequence just heard.

Television ads enable us to do this by providing helps. For example, rhyme is often used. Remember, "Winston tastes good, like a cigarette should." We can remember because of the rhyme. The other day I was watching a television program that caught the audience up to date on the lives of child actors. One such actor starred in the famous Oscar

---

14. Ibid., 11.

Mayer commercial as a child of five and the commercial ran for eighteen years on television. He sang the jingle. "My bologna has a first name, it's O.S.C.A.R.; my bologna has a second name, it's M.A.Y.E.R. Oh I love to eat it everyday and if you ask me why, I'll say, cause Oscar Mayer has a way with B.O.L.O.G.N.A." Notice the rhyme. Not only did the young man, now in his mid-twenties, bring a smile as he sang it again to the audience, but everyone in the audience joined in and sang it too. Organizing the message into a song kept this brand of bologna in the minds of Americans for more than eighteen years! It was a marketing coup.

ASSOCIATION

Association also lends itself to the process of listening. "The extent to which meaning is associated is dependent first on the listener's experience and background and secondly on his ability to use aural context clues. He must be able to anticipate wording as he listens and to confirm or correct in retrospect as he continues to listen. He must be able to 'listen between the words' and capitalize on the speaker's manner of delivery, noting his tone and the mood created."[15]

Mental images come to bear as each word is received. As we share the gospel, there may be words that we use that elicit a response quite unexpected in the listener. If we detect by the listener's facial response that we have "hit a nerve," we need to be sensitive and to ask questions like, "Did I say something that you did not understand?" Never overlook the physical responses of a person when you share your faith. Certain words may have become problematic for the person. He may have attached subjective meanings to the words that remind the listener of a painful personal experience, a joke, a pet name, or a particular friend.[16] Remember, words have

15. Ibid., 12.
16. Ibid., 13.

meaning, and people attach all kinds of meaning to the words you utter. You may be quite innocent, but you also may, in fact, be very offensive.

A few years ago I encountered a fellow worker, whom I respected greatly, at the elevator. She was near retirement age and I was in my mid-thirties at the time. I am from the deep South and she is from Texas. You would think we had a lot in common. However, I greeted her using an endearing phrase that I had heard all my life in church. I said, "Hello, Miss *(first name)*." All my life I had assumed that you could use such a greeting with familiar friends. But she turned on me and retorted, "Don't call me that! Call me Miss *(last name)* or use my first name alone."

I was shocked—so much so, that I kept my distance from her and wrote her a note saying that I was sorry I had offended her. Later that month I got on the elevator with her and another co-worker. He was her age. He made the same mistake. I stood back to watch the fireworks. Sure enough, she hit the ceiling again. He was left with his mouth hanging open when she got off the elevator. It was all I could do not to laugh. We take so much for granted based on our personal experiences. And it sometimes gets us in a tight place!

AUDING

The third step is **auding**, a process by which the continuous flow of words is translated into meaning. Taylor explains that auding involves one or more avenues of thought—indexing, making comparisons, noting sequence, forming sensory impressions, and appreciating.[17]

As each word is recognized it becomes part of the larger spoken message. The listener responds as the flow of words come together. A reaction or response will usually surface as

---

17. Ibid., 6.

the words develop meaning in the listener. Taylor adds that in auding the listener brings into play all of his experience and background and the thinking skills that allow him to index, make comparisons, note sequence, react by forming sensory impressions, or appreciate what is heard.[18]

"Because listening takes time to process and our brains can do other things with the data at the same time, we can project and think ahead even while we are receiving new data."

One of the most interesting abilities that we humans have as we aud, or respond with understanding, is the ability to think ahead. Because listening takes time to process and our brains can do other things with the data at the same time, we can project and think ahead even while we are receiving new data. Taylor points out that in the case of more mature listeners the difference between listening rate and thinking rate may be as great as three or four hundred words per minute.[19]

This is precisely why dialogue is so critical to the gospel presentation. If the witness continues to drone along in the gospel presentation, without any understanding of the other person's ability to think ahead and to anticipate, vital responses and questions will go unheeded. It may be that the person being talked to about the gospel has many questions from the very first words we utter. To ignore her questioning, her thinking ahead, and her responses is to frustrate her. It is helpful to stop often and ask the listener, "Do you have any

18. Ibid., 13.
19. Ibid.

questions?" or "What are you thinking about what I have said so far?" Then listen carefully. The problem with most witnesses is that they have often learned a specific way of presenting the gospel (or of using aids such as a marked New Testament or a tract or a series of questions), that often does not allow the witness the luxury of stopping and asking for responses. And often the witness is prepared in witnessing equipping classes with only the tools necessary to tell and very little instruction on how to listen. A few churches are now trying to correct this problem by carrying people through role-play situations in witness training classes. Questions are asked and situations are demonstrated that highlight the dialogical process needed in the witnessing encounter.

INDEXING

As the person listens, indexing will occur. This is a process where the listener assigns relative values to the information being received. He looks for main ideas and details that separate the relevant from the irrelevant. "For example, in listening to a discussion of safety at school, a student might note those hazards that are most serious and then file away under each type of accident the different ways in which it would occur, its frequency of occurrence, and means of prevention."[20] The person being witnessed to may screen much of what the witness has to say in his presentation. He may, for example, decide that the witness does not really understand his life situation, or that the witness is prejudiced, or that he only uses gender specific language. She will then index accordingly.

Be aware that indexing can occur in the gospel presentation. She may assign value to some aspects of the gospel, but not to others. She may put whole portions of the gospel into categories such as "does not apply." She may accept that

_____

20. Ibid., 14.

people need to be saved, but may not attach any particular relevance to the idea of receiving Christ as personal Lord or the idea of public declaration of faith through baptism.

APPRECIATION

The auding process lends itself to other processes such as making comparisons, noting sequence, and the forming of sensory impressions based on what is heard. One important aspect of the auding process is appreciating. Not too long ago I attended the world-famous Bolshoi ballet in Moscow. Although I have never really been a fan of ballet, the opportunity to go to the Bolshoi was too good to pass up. My appreciation of ballet was enhanced there by the symphony, the audience response (the Russians really like ballet), and the moments of profound silence when facial expression or gentle hand movements carried the bulk of the message of the ballet.

"In responding to the aesthetic nature of a message and its delivery, the listener uses appreciation."[21] Appreciation plays an important part in listening to sermons, plays, poetry, and a vast array of other content. Sometimes the quality of voice, the choice of words, or the clarity of speech lends much to the overall appreciation. A rich resonant voice is more comfortable to listen to than a high-pitched, squeaky one. In the gospel witness, the person sharing should keep in mind the importance of speaking clearly and avoid the tendency to race ahead to the point of decision making. Let the process flow. Take advantage of proper pacing and value the dialogue in such a way that the listener develops appreciation for what he is hearing. Think of yourself as setting a gospel feast before a hungry person. Set the table. Serve each course in the meal with loving care. Allow the person to savor it before the next course is delivered, and observe how

---

21. Ibid., 15.

well he does with it. I ate dinner with a colleague the other day. His young son was with him. The waitress served the young lad some spaghetti and he dived into it, only to put the fork down and declare to the waitress, "I don't wyke dat wed stuff." It may be that the gospel-hungry person has trouble with some of the concepts you are laying before him. Let him react. Help him to cultivate his understanding so that he can fully appreciate the message.

Learning how to listen will make us better tellers of the gospel. As we learn to listen and develop skills in the art of listening, evangelism can become more natural for us. This is because we will move evangelism away from the realm of a sales pitch to the realm of human caring and dialogue that meets needs—among which is the need for salvation, the most important need of all. Don't be misled, however. An evangelism based upon listening to others will cause you to invest yourself in the life of another. It will lead you to risk, to spend time with them, to care. It is not easy. This kind of evangelism will not be satisfied with a hit-and-miss approach. It takes a lot of effort and commitment.

How To Develop Our Listening Skills

How then can we develop the art of listening with both ears? We begin by developing our personal listening skills and then applying what we learn about how we listen to the way we speak to others and how they listen. In the following paragraphs are some suggested exercises to enhance our understanding of the way we listen. You may want to develop your own exercises to enhance your listening ability. Find what works for you and practice developing listening skills of your own.

First, close your eyes. Take several minutes to just listen to sounds around you. Use your mind to search for every sound. Identify it. Then open your eyes and look at the source for every sound. Were you surprised to find that some things are making noise or creating sounds that you usually are not aware of? For example, my computer has a fan on it to cool the power supply. Rarely do I hear it when I am staring at the screen and my fingers are dancing all over the keyboard as they are doing now. But if I close my eyes, I can hear the fan. I am aware of it.

Second, listen to a speech or a sermon or someone reading poetry. Take a pencil and a piece of paper and make a mark for each time you hear a certain word. For example, decide to record the number of times you hear the word "the," or the word "I," or the word "today." By focusing your mind on the process of listening for a particular word, you will train yourself to hear and analyze each word that is spoken.

Third, next time you hear a speech or sermon note the colloquisms, the words that rhyme or the words that are pronounced differently from the way you learned them growing up. Make a list of these words. Write down the sentence. Answer the question, "What can I tell about the person speaking by the words I have written down?" Is she a Northerner, a Southerner, an ethnic, educated or non-educated, ego-centric or caring? What can you determine from what you hear?

Fourth, next time you are driving in your car and you hear a new song on the radio, listen carefully to it. Then turn the radio off and try to hum the tune. Practice this over and over. It will develop your ability to use auditory analysis in listening.

Fifth, practice your ability to organize mentally what you hear. Ask someone to read off to you several ZIP code numbers or telephone numbers. Try to reorganize the numbers in your mind so that you can write them down after a period of a few minutes. Next time you are in church, listen carefully to the pastor's sermon. Do not write down his main points; try to mentally organize them. Then go home and write down as many as you can recall. Practice putting things into categories or attach them to images that will help you re-member.

Sixth, ask someone to read a sentence to you with an unfamiliar word in it. Try to guess what the unfamiliar word means by using the context. Practice this activity over and over to enhance your ability to listen for the context.

Seventh, listen closely to a person talking. Try to iden-tify any sentence spoken that really does not belong to the topic. Ask yourself, "Why was this said? Ask the person who said it. Ask, Is it relevant to the topic at hand?" Learn to spot inconsistencies or contradictions.

Eighth, listen for active words or words that create men-tal images. Jot down words that evoke a response within you. How did those words make you feel? Why did you feel that way? What words can you think of just now that elicit a re-sponse from you, positive or negative? How do you feel when you hear those certain words?

Ninth, critique a speech or sermon. Look for coherent content versus simple random speech. Look for fact rather than opinion. Look for a connection between your experi-ence and what is said. Ask yourself, "Can I believe what this person is saying?" Why? Why not?

Tenth, develop your appreciation skills. Listen to as many good spoken performances as you can. Cultivate oppor-tunities to hear good poetry or good drama. Get away from television programs that produce poor speech, violate good grammar, and are based on nothing more than sensationalism. Look for programs that help mental images to develop in your mind and that evoke responses within you. Paul reminds us to avoid foolish talking, jesting, and the like. It is so easy to pick this pattern up from the television or radio that we need to be careful what we see and hear.

CONCLUSION

Listening is an art. If you desire to be a better witness of the gospel, you must learn to listen to what people are saying, how they say it, and the words they use. Only then can you get to the real truth of how they are receiving the gospel message you are sending them.

All of us cry out for help at some time or another, according to Joyce Huggett.[22] Listening can be an important ministry. "If someone will draw alongside us, recognize that simply to listen is not a waste of time, nor is it less helpful than offering advice or Bible verses, they can provide us with untold support by encouraging us to share our innermost feelings of anxiety or fear or frustration or anger."[23] Little evangelism can take place if we remain insensitive to a person's critical needs.

The caring evangelist will learn to equip herself to be the best listener possible to people's needs. And in that posture all kinds of evangelistic opportunities will avail themselves. Jesus listened to people everyday. He invested Himself in the lives of others. His love for others was demonstrated in the way in which He listened. He listened to meet their needs, whatever they were. We need to learn to listen as Jesus listened.

---

22. Joyce Huggett, *Listening to Others* (Downers Grove: InterVarsity Press, 1988), 87.
23. Ibid.

THINGS TO THINK ABOUT

1. EXPLORE THE CONCEPTS.

Concentrate this week on your listening. Be sensitive to ways in which you hear. Identify sounds that mask your hearing, sounds that are dangers to your hearing, sounds that tire you; sounds that jolt you. Go over in the text all of the factors listed in the process of listening. Discuss them with a friend or with the group of which you are a part.

2. SEARCH THE SCRIPTURES.

Find as many Scriptures as you can that illustrate how persons listened to God. Discuss each one in context. What applications would you draw for today's listening?

3. DISCUSS THE PRINCIPLES.

Why do you think it is important to learn how we listen? Can knowledge of listening techniques cause you to improve the way you respond to people? If so, how?

4. ACT ON WHAT YOU HAVE LEARNED.

Have your hearing tested at a hearing center. Find out how well you respond to certain sounds. If you are in a group, arrange for a hearing expert to test the group's hearing. Analyze your own hearing. In what ways can you identify in your own hearing process the factors listed in the text, such as hearing, efficiency, masking, etc.? Practice this week listening for sounds that you normally ignore. Be sensitive to human speech, its frequency, its variation, its colloquial nature, etc. Determine to be a better listener.

Chapter 4

LISTENING AS JESUS LISTENED

That you may love the Lord your God,
listen to his voice

Deuteronomy 30:20

"These six things doth the Lord hate; yea, seven which are an abomination to Him: haughty eyes . . . " (Prov. 6:16–17). And the list goes on. But the first thing on the list is the proud look—haughty eyes. What does the writer of Proverbs mean?

Simply this: there are certain things that are contrary to God's way and will, and among these is the kind of attitude some people hold toward their fellow human beings, an attitude that says, "You are not important to me."

In the popular movie of 1994, *Schindler's List*, the story is told of Oscar Schindler and his rescue of the Jews during the terrible days of World War II death camps. At one point in the movie, the commandant of the camp is having his coffee and overlooking the camp from the balcony. To the shock of the audience, he picks up a high powered rifle and begins to shoot people who are working in the camp. He sipped his coffee and killed.

The maid in the commandant's house, a Jew, met Oscar Schindler a few days later and broke down before him. She cried uncontrollably. She told Schindler that she feared for her life. She related how she had tried to determine what made the commandant kill with no regard to others. She tried to understand any behavior that might set him off and result her death. But he killed when he was angry, sad or happy. It made no sense. She wept as she seemed to give up trying. At that point, Schindler looked tenderly at her and told her not to worry. "You are important to him," he said. "As long as you are, you will be safe. He kills those who mean nothing to him."

When human life means nothing to others, it becomes easy to kill as the Nazis did. But Jesus died to declare the importance of all persons.

Haughty eyes are the symbol of a life that is enamored with itself—a life that does not take into account the struggles of others. As Hugo Black has said, "In the sunshine of prosperity it is so easy to imagine ourselves people of surpassing merit, and to develop a fine overweening sense of personal dignity which blossoms into either scornful indifference or supercilious disdain."[1]

---

1. Hugo Black, *Listening to God* (New York: Fleming Revell, 1906), 158.

Those who would attempt to barge into a person's life with little or no sympathy for their life's experiences are most assuredly displaying haughty eyes. Certainly Jesus never did this. He shared with others the kingdom of God and its gospel, but He never disregarded them, nor did He become the victim of ego or an attitude of importance. In fact, He played down repeated attempts from the crowds to make Him an earthly king. There are many in our day who should learn this lesson. Of all people, the evangelist ought to be among God's most gentle.

One is reminded of Jesus' gentle approach to people. Little children were drawn to Him like a magnet. Old people, sick people, even the wealthy and important saw in His life a kind of caring that was distinctly different from the rest of humankind. He was not like the religious establishment of His day.

From the very beginning of His ministry, Jesus listened to people. "In the Matthew 18 account, a persistent refrain about listening appears. ("Whoever humble himself like a child. . . ." In a real sense when we are listening to others we are humbling ourselves before them.) Jesus as a twelve-year-old person is portrayed by Luke as being found by His parents in the temple, 'sitting among the teachers, listening to them and asking them questions.'"[2]

As Wayne Oates points out, "This is a clue to His 'silent years,' that is, the years of which we have no record but the one in Luke 2:41–51 as to what His years of personality development were like. We do know that He listened and asked questions."[3]

The importance of others listening to Jesus was announced from heaven to those around Him by God. Mark (9:2–8), Luke (9:28–36), and Matthew (17:1–8) tell of the

---

2. Oates, *The Presence of God in Pastoral Counseling,* 77.
3. Ibid., 78.

transfiguration of Jesus and the voice that came from heaven, "This is my beloved Son, with whom I am well pleased; listen to him."[4]

All through the New Testament, Jesus is one who listened to the needs of others. He engaged people in dialogue and listened to what they had to say. Then He went to the heart of their needs. He engaged them in dialogue and sought to help them understand their need for Him. One familiar story is a case in point.

The Gospel of John records Jesus' encounter with the Samaritan woman at the well of Jacob. The larger issues in this story revolve around everything from ethnic issues (the Jews have no dealings with the Samaritans) to the prohibition of rabbis speaking to a woman in public. But in each of these issues, the listening ear of Jesus met the needs of a woman who came to draw water.

One can well imagine the scene. Jesus' legs were weary. The journey from Judea to Galilee was an especially difficult one. The Pharisees had given Jesus a hard time in Judea. They had hated John the baptizer and now, since Jesus was preaching and many were being baptized, they had turned on Jesus to persecute Him. And so He felt He had to leave Judea.

The hot sun and the journey were not kind, especially at the noon hour. Tired and thirsty, Jesus headed for a well in Sycar of Samaria. Jesus remembered the Old Testament account of Jacob who had given his son Joseph a field and had dug a well there. Maybe there He could refresh Himself.

There came a woman of Samaria to draw water. No doubt their eyes met, if only briefly. She wanted to draw her water quickly and then leave. She was probably a bit concerned upon seeing this man sitting by the well. But her con-

---

4. Ibid.

cern turned to apprehension when she noticed He was a Jew and that now He spoke to her.

"Can you give me a drink?" Jesus asked. He was alone. He probably had nothing to draw water with. His disciples had left Him by the well to go into the town to buy food. Apparently in their haste to get some food they had forgotten to see to His needs.

The woman was startled. "How can you, a Jew, ask me for a drink of water? I am a Samaritan woman. Don't you know that the Jews have nothing to do with Samaritans?"

Jesus knew this woman's need was spiritual. He knew her past. He noticed her slipping out in the heat of the day to draw water when others were resting. He was sensitive to the fact that she could not draw water in the cool of the evening when the other women of the town drew their water. She was an adulteress and lived her life amid the shadows, always avoiding others.

"If you knew the gift of God," Jesus said, "and if you knew me you would have been the one to ask for water. I would have given you living water."

She laughed. "You don't even have anything to draw water with. How can you give me water? This well is deep. Where are you going to get any living water?" Then with a bit of sarcasm she added, "Maybe you think you are greater than our father Jacob who gave us this well. He drank from it, his sons and all his cattle."

Jesus probably smiled as He peered over the edge of the well and felt the coolness of the well in His face. Then He responded. "As long as you and others keep drinking from this well, you will keep getting thirsty. But if you drink the water that I can give you, you will never be thirsty again. In fact, the water that I offer you will be like a spring within you, that will well up even into eternal life."

By now, the woman had taken the water pot off her shoulders. She had drawn closer to Jesus, fascinated with His gentle conversation. Maybe this was the most meaningful conversation she had experienced in a long time. He, she sensed, was not out to use her, as the men in the town did. He seemed really interested in her.

"Sir . . . can you give me this water?" she asked quietly. "I really do not like coming here day after day to draw water in this hot sun."

"Why don't you go and get your husband and come back here?" Jesus suggested.

"I do not have a husband." she responded as she looked away.

"I know" said Jesus. "You have had five husbands. And the one you have now is really not your husband at all. You have been truthful with me."

She backed away from Jesus. Her mind was reeling. The woman did not know what to say, except what seemed obvious. "Sir, you must be some kind of prophet." She felt uncomfortable. She wanted to change the subject.

"Our fathers worshiped on this mountain; and you Jews say that in Jerusalem is the place where men ought to worship. Since you must be a prophet, what is the truth?" she wondered, hoping to redirect His conversation.

Jesus looked at her and addressed her with great respect, "Woman, the hour is coming when worship will not be limited to a mountain in Samaria or Jerusalem. True worshipers will worship the Father in spirit and truth."

"I know the Messiah is coming," she announced to Jesus. "And when He comes He will show us all things. All of this will be made clear."

"I am the Messiah." Jesus said directly.

The woman looked at Him with eyes that met His. Not even the approaching of the disciples could startle her. She was strangely affected by this Jew by the well—so much so that her mind raced with possibilities. "Could this really be the Christ?" she wondered. She could do the only thing that seemed right to do—tell someone else; see if they thought He was the long- awaited One.

Many from the city came to the well to see Jesus. The woman's testimony was so convincing that others wanted to hear Him speak. "He told me all about myself," she told them. There was an excitement in her voice. The more she told them, the more she knew it was real. And others believed also when they talked to Jesus (John 4:1–42).

This story allows the reader to read between the lines. The feel of the story is authentic. It has life and energy. It is not impersonal. It is warm, caring, and dialogical. Jesus took time to listen to the woman, to answer her questions, to get to the bottom of her hurt and need, and to encourage her. In fact, Jesus spoke as often as the Samaritan woman did. "He spoke 175 words (in the Greek text); she spoke 122. This is not unusual in Jesus' personal encounters; He listened as much as He talked."[5] We need to take a lesson from Jesus' style. "Even the Son of God who surely had more to say than could possibly be expressed in His short ministry on earth, took time to listen attentively to undistinguished persons."[6]

The woman who came to draw water in the heat of the day was like a lot of secular people today. She had no personal relationship with God. She knew something about religion, much like the hosts of people in America who say they believe on Jesus but who never attend any church. She may have even been skeptical, thinking that religion had nothing to offer her except ritual. She also knew that she didn't fit. She was an adulteress. People used her. Her hurt was very real. And it seemed to her that no one cared, until Jesus came and asked her for a drink of water. The common need between two human beings for water led to a conversa-

5. Alfred C. Krass, *Evangelizing Neopagan North America* (Scottdale: Herald Press, 1982), 110–11.
6. Masumi Toyotome, "Love Is Listening" in J. Ogden (ed.) *Going Public with One's Faith* (Valley Forge: Judson Press, 1975), 25.

tion that changed her life. Jesus was a master at taking the ordinary things of life around Him, shaping them into meaningful illustrations that pointed others to Him.

Using Silence

The use of silence can be a powerful tool for the listener. Silence, in the midst of noise, can speak more powerfully than words. Henri Nouwen has pointed out that words have lost their creative power. "Their limitless multiplication has made us lose confidence in words and caused us to think, more often than not, 'They are just words.'"[7] Think about it. Aren't your tired of words that are empty, such as "new and improved," "sale," "lifetime guarantee," "a limited time only," and so on.

Here is a real danger to evangelism. We must not be so overbearing when talking to a person that he fails to hear our words. They cease to have meaning to the lost person who has to live in a sea of words every day. Our words concerning eternal life can be drowned unless we know how to become silent and listen to others.

When two people listen to one another, the silence can often be invaded by the presence of Christ, the Eternal Word, in such a way that what were formerly meaningless words, lost among the other meaningless words we hear every day, now take on a new dimension in the quiet recesses of the human heart. Life changes can occur.

Attentive Listening

Swiss Reformed pastor-theologian Eduard Thurneysen speaks of the encounter of the Word of God in conversation with another. He speaks of the pastoral counseling setting suggesting that the goal of counseling is to see to it that the

---

7. Henry J. M. Nouwen, *The Way of the Heart* (San Francisco: Harper, 1981), 46.

counselee is always conscious of his relationship with God. Thurneysen urges pastors to, "listen attentively and at length to the problems of their counselees."[8] Thurneysen rejects all techniques of counseling except that of listening. He says, "If any instruction at all is valid in this area, it would be that one must be prepared to be a listener—a patient, concentrated, attentive, alert, and understanding listener and nothing else."[9]

"From the very beginning of His ministry, Jesus listened to people."

But Thurneysen understands that listening opens the door for the witness. "Listening, for Thurneysen, is always a means to the end of exhorting. The decisive moment in all counseling is what Thurneysen calls, 'the breach in the pastoral conversation.' The conversation is conducted so as to lead to the great pastoral turning point, the disturbing and breaking of the conversation by the hearing of the Word of God."[10] The breech is akin to what Kierkegaard calls, "the leap of faith."[11] It is an encounter with the risen Lord that transforms life. Here is where we must be careful in the witness encounter. We must help the counselee listen as we listen for the speaking of God. We must not be so infatuated with our own words that the Eternal Word fails to have opportunity to speak to the heart of the lost.

This is precisely what I believe to be the problem with many gospel presentations that are done through rote mem-

---

8. Eduard Thurneysen, *A Theology of Pastoral Care* (Richmond: John Knox Press, 1962), 127.
9. Ibid.
10. Edward Thornton, *Theology and Pastoral Counseling,* 49.
11. Ibid.

ory or in a mechanical way. The words related to salvation are pregnant with meaning and implications for the other person's life. And when we utter them, we must learn to be silent and let the Spirit of God drive them home to the mind, heart, and will of the lost person. To hurry through the presentation in order to get to some kind of decision time is to short-circuit God in the process.

Nouwen warns, "When our words are no longer a reflection of the divine Word in and through whom the world has been created and redeemed, they lose their grounding and become as seductive and misleading as the words used to sell Geritol."[12] Jesus knew the value of listening and letting silence be the vehicle by which God thundered His words into the hearts of lost mankind.

A Finger in the Sand

The story is a familiar one, the story of the woman caught in the act of adultery. John 8:2–11 has long been debated as to its inclusion into John's gospel. It appears to be an authentic incident in Jesus' ministry, however, and illustrates the power of silence even in the midst of angry words. Imagine the setting. Let your mind's eye see it.

Early in the morning, Jesus went to the temple. People crowded around Him. They were bees seeking the honey of His presence. So Jesus sat down with them. He probably listened to their stories; He may have laughed with them; but He carefully taught them things they had never heard before.

No small stir began to develop as Jesus' teaching was interrupted. The scribes and Pharisees were dragging a woman toward Jesus. No doubt she was screaming, fighting. The crowd around her was shouting insults. One can picture the scene. They thrust her at Jesus. His eyes may have met hers

---

12. Nouwen, 48.

and locked on to her face. Perhaps after a time the crowd grew silent. A Pharisee must have spoken what they all knew was the just condemnation.

"Teacher, this woman has been caught in the act of adultery. You know our law, Jesus. The law of Moses commands us to stone her. What do you say?" They were trying to tempt Jesus—to catch Him on some technicality of the law—trying to find some way to charge Him with a crime. The crowd grew even quieter.

Jesus captured the moment. Perhaps He decided to let His Heavenly Father thunder the response through the silence. He bent down and wrote in the sand with His finger. You can almost picture the scene as the crowd, puzzled by His behavior, probably began to murmur among themselves. "Look at Him. What's He doing? What is He writing in the sand?"

Many have tried to guess what He wrote. Perhaps He wrote the responses that John attributes to the conversation Jesus had with the woman after her accusers backed away. "Where are your accusers?" Maybe He wrote, "Where is the man?" a question the crowd may not have thought of.

Whatever the case, Jesus used a few moments of writing with His finger in the sand for silence to take over, for Him to listen to His Father and to the crowd. Then Jesus spoke.

"If you are without sin in your life, you may throw a stone at her." Perhaps Jesus bent down again and continued to write and to let the silence take over once again. Conviction tore at the hearts of the listeners in the crowd. They had strained their ears to hear Jesus' response, hoping to catch Him, but instead they heard the voice of God convicting them of their sins. And one by one they stole away from His presence.

Again, there was only silence, only the sound of the woman, her head probably bowed in shame, maybe weeping.

Jesus looked up at her. "Woman, where are the ones who accused you?" he asked.

"No one, Lord." she replied. "No one."

"Neither do I," Jesus said in response. "Go your way. Don't sin anymore." Do you think she believed her ears?

What a powerful demonstration of the way in which Jesus listened to the crowd, to His Father, and to the woman! He turned an impossible situation into an opportunity to tell the crowd of their need for forgiveness also. They had come to Him in righteous indignation. They left Him convicted. The woman came to Him at the point of death and left with a new life.

Would you call these encounters evangelism? Are the encounters ministry? Certainly both evangelism and ministry are merged into a credible witness. Jesus listened and people heard. The dialogue was rather lengthy and involved with the woman at the well, but restrained and quiet with the sinful woman brought before Him. But both lives were changed. "It was as they talked to him that they came to know themselves."[13] That is part of the role of the witness. To help others see themselves, to see Christ, and to see what they can be when they give their lives to Christ. When we help others encounter Jesus in the deep recesses of their souls, that is when transformation occurs. It is often in the darkness of our lives that God is most present. Eugene Lowry tells us to listen to the darkness; see God there.

The lives of many people in the New Testament were filled with darkness and despair, but Jesus was willing to enter their darkness and speak redemptively to it. That is what we are called to do today—to speak redemptively to the darkness around us, to help liberate those caught in it. That will not be done in a quick hit-and-miss approach to evange-

---

13. Frank Lake, *Clinical Theology* (New York: Crossroad Publishing Co., 1966), 2.

lism. It will take an investment of our lives and a willingness to spend a little of ourselves for them. "What made the apostolic band into witnesses was not their ability to comprehend and expound a system of religion, it was their personal knowledge and observation of Jesus Christ himself."[14] Their simple power of observation, their listening to His every word, equipped them to be witnesses. It sensitized them to the way He did ministry, so that all they had to do was to live according to His model.

A VISITOR BY NIGHT

All around us today people are living in the confusion of religious pluralism. From the standpoint of many, the question of who is right is no foregone conclusion. Buddha, Mohammed, Jesus, secularism, New Age? For a lot of people religion is just religion; one is as good as another.

One of the earliest one-on-one evangelistic encounters is found in John 3. There was a confused man of the Pharisees who came to visit Jesus one night. He was as confused theologically as any New Ager today. He had been a ruler of the Jews, responsible for the law, but he was hearing Jesus say things that did not fit his system. He had been disturbed by challenges issued to his basic assumptions about religion and God. So he decided to go to Jesus for some clarification.

"Teacher, I know that you are a teacher from God. After all, your miracles . . . no one could do these great works unless God was with Him," Nicodemus said.

Jesus probably looked Nicodemus right in the eye and got to the real heart of the matter. "I tell you the truth. You will never enter the kingdom of God unless you are born again."

---

14. Ibid.

It is possible to look at this story and miss the intensity of the dialogue. It is easy to assume without a careful reading of the text that Nicodemus came to Jesus because he was interested in giving his life to Jesus; that he came by night because he was afraid his fellow Pharisees would not have understood.

But in reality, Jesus knew his heart. He knew that Nicodemus was a self-righteous Pharisee who had worked hard his whole life at building a religious system that he could control and that could justify him before God. The only problem was that Jesus knew it would not. So Jesus dealt with Nicodemus not as a religious person but as a lost person.

In the course of their dialogue, Jesus confronted Nicodemus's spurious faith, his works-based religion, his Pharisaical righteousness, and his biblical illiteracy.[15]

Nicodemus was taken aback with Jesus' direct response to his flattery. "You must be born again, Nicodemus," Jesus said.

Nicodemus was not naive. He knew that Jesus was not talking about re-entering his mother's body and being born again. In fact, Nicodemus, who had studied the Old Testament all his life, knew that religious teachers and prophets often talked symbolically. He knew that Jesus was saying to him, "You have got to start your religious life all over again, Nicodemus, but this time based on Me and not on yourself."

Sure enough, Nicodemus protested. "How can a man be born when he is old?" What he was really saying was, "I have been in this religion business too long to start all over again. What will everyone think of me? I am a Pharisee. I am not a novice at religion. I have a reputation to think of." You

---

15. John McArthur, *The Gospel According to Jesus* (Grand Rapids: Zondervan, 1988), 38.

can imagine all kinds of protests implicit in his remark to Jesus.

It would be no easy process for Nicodemus. Jesus would be no additional step in his pharisaical process toward heaven. "Far from offering this man an easy conversion, Christ challenged him with the most difficult demand He could make. Nicodemus would gladly have given money, fasted, or performed any ritual Jesus could have prescribed. But to call him to spiritual rebirth was asking him to acknowledge his own spiritual insufficiency and turn away from everything he was committed to."[16]

I can imagine that Nicodemus's face was flushed. Jesus pressed him harder. "How is it that you cannot understand this?" Jesus asked, "Aren't you *the* teacher of Israel?" Jesus asked recognizing Nicodemus's reputation as the preeminent teacher of the day. Nicodemus was one teacher who was left with nothing more to say.

The point of illustrating this story is the proactive way that Jesus approached Nicodemus. With the woman at the well Jesus met a need. He did it by answering questions and by an extended conversation as He relaxed. With the woman caught in adultery Jesus showed compassion and instruction for her to go and sin no more. But Jesus demonstrated a philosophical and theological approach to the dialogue with Nicodemus. Different dialogues are appropriate with different persons. Dialogue does not imply chit-chat. Dialogue can be direct, to the point, challenging, and heavy with content.

Nicodemus did not need a friendly theological chit-chat. He needed to confront his own idolatry: his self-righteousness, and his feeling of security within his own religious system. Witnessing to a cult member, a person from a world religion, or an agnostic may involve hard questions and intense dialogue. It may cause us to dig deeper into the

---

16. Ibid., 40.

Scriptures and to bring much more light on the lost person's spiritual state than might be necessary perhaps with others. Jesus listened to people and sized up their situation, often based on what they said to Him. You and I need to carefully listen to the other person's life story. She may be like the woman at the well, looking for security, moving from one hurt to another. He may be like the woman caught in adultery, indulging in the lusts of the world. She may be searching, but in the wrong place, like Nicodemus. If you and I listen to others and ask the Holy Spirit of God to speak to our heart, and give us insight into the other person's life story, we can develop more confidence in our ability to point them to Jesus. We have to care enough to listen.

Recently I heard a radio preacher tell a story that tore at my heart. A young boy of fifteen ran away from home, but he left his parents a note. The note went something like this.

Dear Mom and Dad,

Don't worry about me. I am in another city now and I am living in a shelter. I am going to get myself a job and start a new life. I simply could not keep on living with you anymore. I still love you because you are my parents. So don't ever doubt that. But I needed what I guess you could never give to me.

You see, Mom and Dad, I needed you to listen to me. I would often come to you, Dad, and I would want you to let me tell you about my day, about my friends, and about my troubles. But you were always tired. You always came home from work, ate dinner, and plopped down in front of the TV. When I came around you never looked at me. You just read your paper and watched the games on the tube.

And mom, you were always talking on the phone to your friends. I would need to talk to you but you would scold me for interrupting your phone calls. And you went shopping all the time. You bought me nice things. They were OK for a while, but then I got tired of them. All I really wanted was you.

So, Mom and Dad, you go on and live your life without me. I am going to be all right. I have so much to tell someone about myself. So I am going to find me someone who will listen.

Love,

Your son

The streets in most major cities are full of people who need someone to listen to them. People who live in the house next door need someone to listen to them. Persons who work with you and me need someone to listen to them. It is very easy for us to form tightly knit circles of friends with whom we carry on dialogue. Sociologically our need to communicate with others can be satisfied within these circles of just a few people who do not threaten us or challenge us beyond our wishes, and with whom we know the boundaries. But as Christians we are called ever to widen our circles of influence. Acts 1:8 tells us that we will be witnesses not only at home where it is safe, but to the ends of the earth where we must take risks. We should not shy away from daily encounters with strangers where opportunities to speak to others and engage them in conversation about Christ can take place. Churches who claim to know of no prospects are made up of Christians who simply have not learned to carry the gospel into everyday life beyond their tightly knit circle of friends, to a world where they will be challenged to listen the way Jesus did. Lord, help us to expand our opportunities and learn to listen to others the way You listen to us.

THINGS TO THINK ABOUT

1. EXPLORE THE CONCEPTS.

Read through the gospels and note how Jesus listened to others. Think about your personal style of listening. Do you listen as Jesus did? Are you interested in the other person or in your own agenda? Be honest in your appraisal of your listening habits.

2. SEARCH THE SCRIPTURES.

Find as many examples as you can that illustrate how Jesus dealt with people through dialogue and listening. List the passage and write a brief description of the characteristics of the situation. Note differences and similarities.

3. DISCUSS THE PRINCIPLES.

Discuss with a friend what listening to another implies about the other person's worth in your eyes. How do you use silence? Discuss with a friend or in a group how silence makes you feel. What are creative ways to use silence?

4. ACT ON WHAT YOU HAVE LEARNED.

Go to your church or to a retreat and spend an afternoon in silence. Pray, think, and listen to God. Ask God to give you new insights about silence and to show you how you can apply listening skills in the life of a specific person who is lost.

Chapter 5

DIALOGUE VS. MONOLOGUE

Wherefore, my beloved brethren,
let every man be swift to hear, slow to speak.

James 1:19, KJV

We grow up listening to sounds that eventually translate into meaning. As adults we listen for the first words that our children speak. How wonderfully we strain our imagination to take the first sounds of a child and interpret them "mama" or "dada." Soon we are no longer satisfied to hear single words. We long for phrases, for sentences, the stuff of communication. We speak and our children learn to speak back. Monologue turns to dialogue, though even in the simplest form.

The power of speaking, of being at center stage, in the vortex of attention while others listen, has an intoxication, a dynamic all its own. James Hilt has pointed out that persons absorbed in what they want to say all the time are usually obsessed with how they are coming across rather than with the message itself. It is directly related to their own self image. "In their minds listening just doesn't draw the same attention and esteem from others that speaking does."[1]

Dialogue, however, sets the stage for an entirely different mode of communication. A different dynamic exists. For one thing we are more vulnerable to others when we are in the dialogical mode. The actors on the stage are in different dramas. In this dialogical drama there is humor, sadness, empathy, joy, and a host of other emotions not usually found in a monological mode. Each emotion shifts the stage and the situation. This changing of the stage, a change in the focus of attention, is what is to be explored in this chapter.

What happens when the witness encounter moves from one stage to another stage, where the stage props are different and the scenery is no longer applicable when monologue shifts to dialogue? What roles do the actors play? More importantly, how does the listener change? What is the role of the Holy Spirit in monologue and dialogue? Do barriers to communication go up or do they come down when monologue shifts to dialogue?

The witness whose agenda is to get the message across at all costs has not simply violated his listener. His real problem is that he has not learned how to effectively listen to God. Yet so many times people are trained to witness by only learning **their** lines. They have no appreciation for the lines of the other player in this drama called life.

---

1. James Hilt, *How to Have a Better Relationship with Anybody: A Bible Approach* (Chicago: Moody Press, 1984), 55.

During a summer in the sixties I was assigned to be a part of a music/drama summer missions team. Our task was to go to campgrounds and churches around the Myrtle Beach, South Carolina, area and perform religious drama and give concerts. There were seven of us who spent several weeks learning lines for four different dramas we were to perform.

I played various parts in the dramas. Once I was a soldier. Then I was a traveler. Then I was a king. And so on it went. In each play, I had to learn not only my lines but the lines of each player in the drama. Otherwise, I would not know when it was my time to speak. The other players also learned my lines. This came in handy a few times when we temporarily forgot our lines or stumbled over a line of dialogue in the nervousness of performing. The other players could whisper a line or help a struggling actor get started again.

Knowing each others lines also provided for a few inside jokes and special moments for the cast. We tried hard to twist a line or a phrase in such a way playfully to cause our team members to laugh in an otherwise serious moment. This kept us mentally alert and sharp. It forced us to get deeper into our characters for security. Participating on the drama team helped us as individuals get to know one another better onstage and offstage. Being in a play taught me a lot about the process of communication and about other people.

THE DRAMA OF LIFE

To a degree we are all in the drama of life. We share lines with each other all the time: over coffee, at lunch, in the hall, and at play. How we react to each others' lines makes the day enjoyable or very tense and unpleasant for us . The witnessing encounter also should be seen as a process of sharing not only in the drama of life but in knowing the other person.

Effective evangelism takes into account the other person's point of view. The problem with an evangelistic witness that is only a monological expression is that the spotlight is upon only one player in the drama. Life is much more interesting than that, just as a drama is more interesting with many players than just one. Further, as Matthew 22:34–40 points out, we are exhorted to love the Lord God with all our heart and the second great commandment is to love others as much as we love ourselves. If we truly love others we will invest in them. We will listen to understand them. We will not commit the sin of idolatry, that is, believing that we are the center of the universe and that all others should always listen to us. We will be compelled to honor that other person's point of view. "The fact that many Christians are poor listeners tells me that they are clearly failing with the second most important task given us. Unwilling to shake loose from their self-centered tendency toward monologue, they too, along with unbelievers, contribute to the dialogue of the deaf."[2] That is, they talk so much that others quit listening to them and to their message. We have too important a message to proclaim to risk others turning a deaf ear to us. Christ did not talk and talk and talk. He listened far more than He talked.

"Here was a Man who was given the most important mission in history. Yet, Jesus repeatedly took time to listen intently and patiently to individuals, even when passing through suffocating crowds. He was never too busy to stop and listen."[3] James Hilt points out that in Christ's post-resurrection encounter with two disciples on their way to Emmaus (Luke 24:13–33), it becomes clear that He was an

---

2. Ibid., 56.
3. Ibid.

excellent listener. Christ was not preoccupied with Himself. "He had just experienced barbaric torture on the cross and was freshly risen from the grave. Nevertheless, He was truly absorbed in what the two others felt and had to say."[4] Jesus asked probing questions. This was His style from the earliest days as a child to His death on the cross. Even in pain on the cross, He sought to hear from His Father in Heaven. Jesus did not manipulate others. He was not interested in surface comments or in shallow responses. He wanted to know what made people think and act the way they did. He asked the disciples, "Whom do men say that I am?" He wanted to be sure that they were understanding His mission. I am afraid that we sometimes want a decision from people more than we want to be sure they understand the message that drove us to share with them in the first place. I am convinced that when we witness to others we must spend much time asking them questions about what we are saying to them. We must make sure they are clearly understanding our message. And above all, we must constantly be listening to the Heavenly Father as He directs us throughout the whole encounter.

While on the drama team, I learned how important the director's job is. She often helped us with simple expressions and interpretations that enhanced the believability of our characters. She told us when we were being too timid or when we were too overpowering. In many ways, the Holy Spirit of God is the director in the witnessing drama. The Spirit enables us to be sensitive to the other person and to listen to their life story, to laugh with them, cry with them, and to know when they are needing to plunge deeper into the process of exploring faith.

If we leave God out of the process or ask the Holy Spirit's blessing only when we get into trouble in the witnessing encounter, we become much like the performer who stands

---

4. Ibid.

on the stage paying no attention to the director. Just off stage the director may be signaling that the actor has forgotten an important line in the drama or has come into the scene too soon. It could spell disaster for the drama. When the witness enters an encounter with another person and lays out his memorized speech from, "Do you know you are going to heaven when you die?" to "Why don't you give your life to Jesus?" with hardly a breath in between, he may be ignoring the direction of the Holy Spirit who could be signaling the witness that he has come on too strong.

James Hilt suggests several ways to enhance our listening skills throughout the witnessing process. These are based upon Hilt's understanding of the way Jesus dealt with others.[5]

First, become genuinely interested in others and their life story. Do not worry about how you are coming across or try all the time to build your image with that person. Go beyond yourself and seek to get involved with the other person. Determine to end any tendency toward self-centered monologue.

Second, develop the art of asking probing questions. Ask creative questions that take you beyond the obvious. Try to glean from the other person insights they are developing based upon what you say to them. Find out how deeply your evangelistic witness is going into their soul.

Third, while you are asking probing questions, make sure the other person knows that you are not rushing her. Don't keep a stopwatch on the occasion. If time runs out, make plans to continue at another time. Give time to speak and then give time to listen. You will find that silence will be an ally in the process. Remember Philip stayed in the chariot as long as he needed to in order to help the eunuch understand the gospel.

---

5. Ibid., 57.

SILENCE IS GOLDEN BUT ALSO EFFECTIVE

In the witnessing process the witness must be a listener through the silence. She must stop at times and dialogue in silence with the other person. Like being in a play, the witness must speak and then wait. Be silent.

Through the witness encounter many serious words are spoken. Many demands are made. It takes time to process the severity of Christ's demands, His requirements of our lives. We often do not allow time to let the implications fully sink into another person's consciousness. Being silent at times, giving pauses a chance to minister to the person, the Holy Spirit can reinforce what we are saying in the heart and mind of the hearer.

Learning to wait on the other person to respond is vital.

Times of silence, pauses in the encounter, can slow the pace and cause us as witnesses really to look at the person, to consider her life, to value her as a person, to feel compassion. The Holy Spirit can use that time to soften our hearts so that we will be even more caring in our witness. It may be that in these moments when we are bathed in the presence of God, the witness hears the still small voice of God most clearly. It can become evident that God is doing a work in the silence, that the lost person is dealing with issues and connecting to the power of God in her life. It may be that the lost person is being encouraged by the Holy Spirit and filled with receptivity to the gospel in ways never experienced before.

Learning to wait on the other person to respond is vital. Otherwise the witness can miss important clues, given by the other person during the silence, to a misunderstanding, need for clarification, or confusing response to what is being said. Wayne Oates has said that silence can uncover what speech would otherwise hide.[6]

The person who always strives to make a gospel presentation universal in its sharing forgets the model of Jesus. He presented the gospel of the kingdom in many contexts. The point is that one who speaks and never listens, who is intent on getting his message across without dialogue, may be signaling that he really does not need God in the process at all. He may be relying upon *his* message, *his* skill in presenting the gospel, or *his* manner for power, direction, effect, and result. This is not to say that God does not speak even in the midst of those who are intent on getting the message across at all costs. He often does, just as the director sometimes whispers the actor's lines, lowers the curtain, changes the scene or sends another actor on stage to avoid disaster. But why take the chance? Why not include the Holy Spirit's direction from the very first words that are spoken?

We would be better witnesses if we could learn to listen to people. But listening to people takes time and we are busy people. So, our models of gospel presentation allow mostly for presentation, not listening.

The witness encounter has to make provision for time to talk and time to listen. The encounter needs pauses as surely as our hearts need rest between each beat. The pauses enable us to listen to God. The very fact that many witnessing programs teach us to carry along another person to pray while we are talking portrays the need for someone to be listening to God. It may be helpful to have someone else there to pray for the encounter, but the presenter also needs to be praying throughout the process. He can only do that effectively as he pauses, dialogues, and listens to God and to the other person.

---

6. Wayne Oates, *The Presence of God in Pastoral Counseling* (Dallas: Word Publishing, 1986), 70.

We are so result-oriented that we often do not allow enough time in the process for God or for listening to Him.

As we listen however, something wonderful happens. The chart below explains.

GOD

Lost may speak to God

God speaks

Witness may not hear God

Witness does all the talking

Little or no response from lost

Lost Person   **Witness**

Monological Witness Process
with little dialogue or listening

In a monological process God can speak to the lost person. The lost may even speak to God in silent prayer. But if the witness is so intent upon getting a decision, he may focus so entirely on the lost person and the message that he doesn't hear God speaking. How can he? He is too busy talking.

A dialogue allows God to speak between the pauses. God can speak to the witness. He can speak to the lost person. The lost person may speak to God. The lost person can ask questions of the witness and the witness can respond led of God. If this process is followed the witness encounter has the opportunity to reflect the heart and mind of God as He speaks to the witness, giving him direction as He cultivates the heart of the listener. Learn to listen to God. Listen to Him

speak in the encounter. Listen to your own heart as you witness. Hear God giving you direction. Dialogue with your
heart. Dialogue with the other person. Help her begin talking
and listening to God. Such a witnessing encounter may take
more time but in the long run will plant the gospel deeper
into a seeking heart..

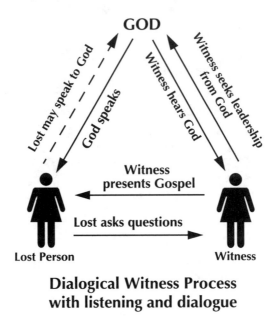

**Dialogical Witness Process
with listening and dialogue**

At least one church in Louisville, Kentucky, has imple-
mented an approach to outreach through listening support
groups. They believe that listening to people can make a bigger impact than preaching to them.[7] The church has formed
groups that listen to people who are dealing with cancer,
heart problems, grief, and alcoholism. The weekly discussion groups are loosely structured and provide an open, yet
confidential forum where feelings can be shared openly. The
church believes these groups are a natural setting for holistic

7. Melanie Childers, "Church Preaches by Listening Through Support Groups,"
The Western Recorder (March 10, 1992), Vol. 166, No. 10.

ministry to people who have no one else to listen to them or provide support for them. The groups have led to reaching outside the church and ministering the gospel to people who otherwise would not participate in church life.

Often people make an easier transition into faith when they find others who will listen to them. They see that the person actually cares for them. They do not feel like a target of someone's evangelical sales pitch.

If saving transformation is to take place in a person's life, that lost person needs to touch the faith of a child of God. Only then will he know it is real. A few years ago, I was interim pastor in a very small church. One Sunday morning a man walked into the church. From where I sat on the podium I could see that he was ragged and dirty. He nearly fell as he slipped into a back pew. I felt that he was probably intoxicated. Nevertheless I proceeded with the service. At the end of the service I went immediately to him. The smell of alcohol was strong. He and I talked for quite some time as people in the church left. No doubt many in the church were offended by his presence.

He asked me to visit him sometime. I agreed. We set an appointment the next day for me to visit his home. I told him I would be there. I asked him to promise he would not drink before I came so that we could perhaps communicate a little better. He agreed.

The next day, at the appointed hour, I visited his home. He was sitting outside on the porch. When I approached he seemed very surprised. "I never figured you'd come," he said. "Why not?" I asked. "Cause all the other preachers who promised me they would come to my house never did," he replied. He began to tell me his story.

For over an hour I listened. Very gently I interacted with his story and led him to talk about his spiritual life. I asked him who God was in his life. He kept on talking. Finally, he turned to me and said, "You know, preacher, I am no good to God. I been too bad. I'm lost and that's all I will ever be," he confessed.

This opened the way for me to illustrate a couple of stories from the Scripture of others who were like him, who had no hope. Then I told him about Jesus and that Jesus wanted to restore him and love him. And I told him that I wanted to see him well and whole again also. Then I listened to his questions.

Never once did I give him some kind of pre-packaged gospel. It would not have worked for him. He had told me that once before someone had visited him and tried to get him saved. He had told them he was not interested. But he sensed that I really did care. He trusted me.

As I told him about Jesus, tears swelled into his eyes. When I told him that he was not too bad to keep God from loving him, he cried openly. Then he said to me, "Can I give my life to Jesus now?" We both fell to our knees and I led him to pray and then invited him to pray his own prayer. When we finished I could see in his face that a burden had been lifted off him. He was transformed, he had honestly prayed for God to transform or save him. He asked Christ into his life. And I know that Christ honored his prayer. The love of Christ broke into his miserable situation and saved him from despair here on earth and eternal hell. Had I not listened to him and loved him, he might never have responded to the love of God. I believe he touched the love of God through me as I was willing to listen to him and honor his life struggles with time enough to care.

In that kind of context we can be the best evangelists and best share the story of a God who, "loved humans enough to die for them . . . to transform persons and awaken in them the memory of who they, too, were created to be. The transforming faith of conversion is a response of amazement to God's love which results in love for others."[8] We can never properly demonstrate that love of God unless we take time to listen to others, for listening enhances the presence of God in our lives and in the lives of those who are engaged with us in a gospel dialogue.

THE PRESENCE OF GOD THROUGH LISTENING

In the New Testament there are numerous dialogues recorded. We have looked at a few. But none are quite as telling as those that center around our Lord. The presence of God is demonstrated in the life of Jesus as He engaged in dialogue with others and as He listened to them.

In Luke 2 Jesus is sitting among teachers and talking with them. He listens and asks probing questions. Luke 2:47 tells us that the ones who heard Jesus were astonished at His understanding and His answers. No doubt Jesus' dialogue was made even more powerful as He listened and responded with insight gained from His Father. He did not lecture the teachers. He respected them and He demonstrated His respect by paying close attention to their insights.

One does not get the impression that this young lad, the Son of God, forgot that in their human eyes He was but a mere child. It was all the more important if God was going to break into that gathering for Jesus to respond, led by His Father, to the questions they asked of Him. Evidently His answers touched them where they needed to be touched because Luke says they were astonished. Those who believed they knew all they needed to know about God were brought face to face with Him in the presence of this young lad.

The presence of God the Father is manifested in passages in Mark 9:2–8, Luke 9:28–36, and Matthew 17:1–5, as Peter, James, and John are taken to a high mountain and there they are enveloped with the presence of God in a cloud. There God focuses their attention on Jesus and exhorts the

8. Newton H. Malony and Samuel Southard, *Handbook of Religious Conversion* (Religious Education Press,).

disciples to listen to Jesus. The disciples, though on the mountain in the very presence of God, failed to understand what was happening. We can also fail in our witnessing task unless we learn to expect the presence of God and prepare for His presence in our witnessing encounters.

The Roman centurion saw the presence of God in the last moments of Jesus' life. Matthew 27:54 records the centurion's statement, "Truly this was the Son of God." He had seen Jesus' behavior on the cross. He had seen Him in pain, yet he saw Jesus talking to His mother and others around the foot of the cross. He had seen Jesus talking to His Father about the sins of the crowd and asking forgiveness for them. He had observed Jesus' sensitivity to the lostness of the thief on the cross beside Him and His willingness to listen to his plea for mercy and for remembrance when Jesus came into His kingdom. He saw Jesus seek solace from His father. He saw all the events of the day and watched a man die as no other man had died before. The presence of God through Jesus made a powerful impression on this lost centurion. Others are watching our lives and our witness to see if they see God in us. In every witness encounter you and I must understand that the biblical goal is to get others to listen to Jesus, to understand who He is, to be reconciled to Jesus, and to let Him redirect lives and re-mold lives. The presence of God is promised to us as witnesses where two or three of us are gathered in His name—wherever we are caring for others, telling them about Jesus, and seeking to minister in loving ways to them. Jesus promises to be with us, but we must pay attention to His presence there. We must listen to Him and to one another so that the communion of spirit that He promised will be evident to all present.

THINGS TO THINK ABOUT

1. EXPLORE THE CONCEPTS.

Be honest about your feelings about yourself. Are you a confident person, an arrogant person, a humble person? How would you describe yourself? How does James Hilt's quote in chapter 4 apply to your situation? Are you absorbed in yourself or a giving person? Do you find it easy to engage in dialogue, or do you need always to be talking?

2. SEARCH THE SCRIPTURES.

Examine dialogue in the Scriptures. Meditate upon Jesus' encounter with the woman at the well. How would you describe the dynamics of the situation? How did Jesus feel? How did the woman feel?

3. DISCUSS THE PRINCIPLES.

Talk with a friend or in your group about dialogue and monologue in everyday life. Examine your lifestyle. If you give orders each day, or talk a lot each day to persons, how would you evaluate your ability to listen? If you listen a lot or dialogue with others a lot, how would you evaluate your ability to present the gospel in a short time frame?

4. ACT ON WHAT YOU HAVE LEARNED.

Pray for God to lead you in the coming week to be aware of His presence as you dialogue with others and as you listen to them. Keep a notebook of your observations and the opportunities you have to say a word about Christ in the normal course of conversation and daily activities.

Chapter 6

WHAT PEOPLE DON'T SAY

"When I spoke, no one listened."

Isaiah 66:4

The communication process would be a whole lot easier if each of us had a video display attached to our foreheads. That way the listener could view what was going on in our mind before actually speaking the words we hear. It could be quite comical to view a person's thoughts before she said them. We might view a lot of inconsistency. Have you ever caught yourself saying something entirely different from what you meant? Do you ever feel verbally dyslexic?

The process of communication is a complex one. That's why it is hard to listen. "Douglas Steere describes the intricate difficulty of listening: 'A Finn once suggested to me that in every conversation between two people there are always at least six persons present. What each person said are two; what each person meant to say are two more; and what each person understood the other to say are two more.'"[1] The next time you are talking to another person and listening to what she is saying, remember that these six people are present.

GATHERING THOUGHTS

Most of us gather thoughts together, process them into sentences, and then say them. It is a complicated process. Try this exercise. The next time you are listening to someone, or better yet, in a lively debate, look at the speaker's eyes. Chances are when they are trying to gather thoughts together their eyes will glance around the room. But when the thought is fairly well processed, then bang, they will focus their eyes on yours and lock on, if only for an instant, and they will say what they have pulled together as a response. You had better learn to pay attention to someone when they look you straight in the eye. That's usually when they are dead serious about what they believe.

This whole string of ideas being processed by the mind is like a train, although a lot more complicated. Each car on the track represents a thought that is loaded with an emotional response.

Consider the following dialogue for example: John comes home from work. He drives up with the kids from the day care. As Mary, who has just gotten home only a few minutes before John, looks out the window, it is evident by the

---

1. Wayne Oates, *The Presence of God in Pastoral Counseling* (Dallas: Word Publishing, 1986), 79.

look on John's face that his day has been pretty tough. He just looks tired.

The kids run into the house. Mary greets the kids and then in walks John.

"Hi, honey!" A tired embrace. "Tough day, huh?"

John mumbles something under his breath. (Obviously the train on the track isn't moving yet, but the steam is building in the boiler.)

He settles down into his easy chair. Mary goes into the kitchen to see what to cook for dinner. Later that evening, after dinner, both get a few minutes to talk together. John still seems preoccupied, so Mary asks again.

"Everything go OK at work today?"

Now the train starts rolling.

"Not exactly."

"You want to talk about it?" (Secretly Mary wants to tell John about her tough day too, but he seems to be really in need of a little extra care. So Mary doesn't tell John about her obnoxious boss who treats her like a slave. Instead, she tries to help John feel a little better.)

He shifts in his chair. He seems to almost snap out of his dull trance and looks right into Mary's eyes.

"You remember that guy, Bill, who's always late with his reports. . . . ?"

Now the train is definitely moving down the track.

"That rascal never does his work. I cover for him all the time. And guess who is up for promotion?"

Anyone around can hear the whistle blow. The train is not just moving. It's screaming down the track. And with every sentence, each boxcar of emotional baggage on that train is unloaded. Even the neighbors could see the emotion. A casual observer might even feel the hurt. All that cargo translates not only into words but into physical response as well. Nerves tense. The heart races. Blood pressure elevates.

Veins swell. Adrenalin courses through John's body. He's ready for a fight.

"If I had my way about it, I'd fire that Bill. That's what I'd do."

The caboose. Little wonder people have heart attacks.

EMOTIONAL BAGGAGE

But what happens when you and I hear the issues and ignore the fact that boxcar #1 is loaded with dynamite set to go off? Or if we lock onto boxcar #3 but find it is loaded with only a firecracker? The emotional baggage underlying each point is as important as the point being made. Sometimes when we notice a person is upset by what he says, we misunderstand that there is often a whole layer of issues driving his complaints. Divorces are made of this kind of stuff. And it happens every day. People pay a lot of attention to the words being said, but often ignore the emotional baggage that drives the language.

The opposite is just as true. Joyful language is also driven by the emotional responses in a person. The body can react to joyful dialogue also. If the issue is one of joy, for example, the body can get very relaxed. The heart rate can go down. Blood pressure can decrease.

When you and I listen to people talk, do we observe what is underneath the language? If we don't, we can often miss opportunities to get at the real issues. When someone says "No!" to the gospel, are we offended? Or do we try to look deeper into why that person responded that way? What emotional baggage might that person be carrying? Did he have one of those days when nothing went right? Is he too content and happy right now to sense a need for God?

HOW WE MIGHT BE HEARD

In evangelistic listening it is important to hear what people do *not* say when the evangelist tries to elicit a response regarding the gospel message. Without an opportunity to listen to them the dialogue may flow a little like the following:

"Hi, my name is Ron."

"Hello, I'm Phil." (Oh, no. Another preacher coming to visit me and lay a guilt trip on me.)

"Phil, I'm from Too Busy to Listen to You Church and I'd like to know if you've ever thought about being saved?"

"I'm not sure." (Give me a break fellow. Can't you see the baseball game is on TV?)

Obviously, this is an extreme and hopefully ridiculous example. Or is it? How many times do we visit people and try out our routines on them before we ever get around to actually engaging them in meaningful dialogue? How often do we lead them to follow our agenda in a witnessing conversation?

That person may be very busy. He might not feel well. She might have just suffered some trauma. The person may be mentally exhausted. If the witness is unaware of the circumstances, yet plunges ahead with some kind of rigid presentation, not much is likely to happen. What would happen in the above example in the care of a sensitive, listening evangelist? Perhaps the dialogue might go like this:

"Hi, my name is Ron and I'm from I'd Like to Listen to You Church."

"Hello, my name is Phil." (Oh, no. Another preacher coming to visit me and lay a load of guilt on me.)

"Phil, I know I'm infringing on your time tonight, but our church was just out meeting people in the area and we did not want to miss seeing you. If this is not a good time, please let me know and I'll be glad to come back at another time."

"Well, I was watching the baseball game." (Yea, right. Now watch him ignore what I said and hang around anyway.)

"OK, Phil. I understand. Here's a little brochure about our church and a word about how you can know Jesus as your Savior if you do not already. I want to leave it with you. Enjoy the game. I hope I can see you again soon. Take care."

As Ron leaves, Phil can't believe what he has just seen and heard. (He really did leave. Maybe he's different from the rest of them. Hey, I wonder how the Braves are doing?) He hurries back to the game, but I'll bet during the commercials he will pick up the brochure Ron left. "Yeah, there it is on the coffee table." And I'll bet he will look a little closer at it. What kind of impression did Ron leave? Will he get in the door next time he comes by Phil's house? Do you think they might strike up a conversation next time? An old saying goes like this, "A person will sit up and notice you if you will sit up and notice what makes him sit up and notice."

There is certainly nothing wrong with respecting another person's space. Donald Soper said, "We must begin where persons are, rather than where we would like for them to be."[2] Jesus was the master of noticing everything about people and their life situations. While others watched the world rush by in a blur, Jesus noticed Nathanael, deep in thought, under the fig tree. He noticed Matthew, intense, industrious, and diligent, even though the rest of the town ignored him. He noticed Zacchaeus, curious, lifting himself above the crowd to get a glimpse, when the rest of the people would have crowded him out. He saw a blind beggar beside the road

---

2. Delos Miles, *How Jesus Won Persons* (Nashville: Broadman Press, 1982), 55.

outside of Jericho needing someone to help him.[3] Jesus knew
the important of context.

WITNESSING AND CONTEXT

The context of a witnessing encounter calls for sensitivity on our part. Context can become a major part of the par-
ticipant's interpretation in the witnessing encounter. The
context of the witnessing situation may cause the person to
shy away from listening to a gospel presentation. Have you
ever tried to witness to a waitress who is busy waiting tables
in a restaurant? The context doesn't lend itself to much more
than handing her a gospel tract, certainly not a thirty-minute
discussion. At other times the context may be very appropriate. You may find the person quite willing to engage with
you in meaningful dialogue about the gospel.

A few years ago, Southern Baptists held their annual
convention in Las Vegas. It was not a very likely meeting
place for a group of people who do not gamble, drink, nor engage in most of what Las Vegas stands for. The decision was
deliberately made to go there and hopefully leave the town
somewhat different from the way it normally was. One of the
events in the week's activities was the witnessing encounter
known as "Crossover Las Vegas." This was an event marked
by teams of witnesses going door-to-door introducing people
to Southern Baptists and to Christ. A good friend and I went
together on our assignment. We were to visit fifty homes in
an afternoon. In spite of the heat of the afternoon, we set out
on our assignment. I shall never forget the experience. While
many people were cordial, some were less than cordial to receive us at their door. I remember one man who slammed the
door in our face when we told him we had come to talk to
him about his faith.

---

3. Miles, *How Jesus Won Persons,* 86.

But among those who were cordial, one person stuck out. When we told him we were Southern Baptists, he beamed, "I have been expecting you." This shocked us until he told us what he meant. It seems that he had been impressed with the advertising he saw on television about the Southern Baptists coming to Las Vegas. He had noticed the billboards. He had gotten the mail-outs from churches and had heard ads over the radio. He was prepared for our visit. And we had a nice visit from him. He thanked us for coming.

"Remember, there is a significant difference between how the message is received when others are on your turf and when you are on theirs."

The context for this man had been set. He had been prepared to receive us, and thus, we entered into dialogue with him with a high degree of receptivity on his part. It is important to note that context, like words, gestures, and the like, both facilitate and restrict the messages they intend to convey.[4] I expect that the man who slammed the door in our face had seen the ads also, but he had apparently been turned off by them and the whole notion that the Baptists were coming!

Context in the witnessing encounter cannot be ignored. It can fog up the encounter to such an extent that regardless of what you try to say, it will not be heard. On the other hand, the context might make the sharing much easier. Remember, there is a significant difference between how the message is received when others are on your turf and when you are on theirs.

---

4. Charles H. Kraft, *Communication Theory for Church's Witness* (Maryknoll: ORBIS Books, 1991), 132.

As people become more private, for example, the context of witnessing in the home may become more difficult. It used to be that churches could enter almost any neighborhood or apartment complex, but now the situation has changed. Laws prohibit the exercise of religion in some contexts. I heard the other day where a man was stopped for preaching on a street corner because a merchant nearby objected to the noise and called the police. Christians are going to be forced to consider the context of the witnessing situation more carefully as this nation infringes more and more upon religious liberty. Certain groups have as an agenda to expunge every expression of religion from public life in this nation. It is interesting to note that the Constitution prohibits the establishment of a state religion, not the free exercise of religion. Yet this continues to be misinterpreted by groups that have as their agenda the secularization of America. These groups are ignorant of our history. They need to go back and examine the lives and writings of the founders of this nation. They will find a dependence upon God and desire to have a Christian nation as the intended bedrock of this country.

Jesus was an expert in understanding context. He went to the home of some people, such as Zacchaeus (Luke 19:1-10). He went to eat with sinners. He visited the synagogues and the temple. He escaped to lonely places to instruct His disciples and to commune with the Father. In each situation Jesus communicated differently and according to the context. He made it clear to a rich young ruler that his wealth stood in his way to life eternal, and to another that her faith in the midst of a crowd had made her whole. He listened and responded to each agenda.

We are not always able to control the context. Sometimes we will be called upon to speak a word of witness in the midst of wealth or in a crowd. At other times we may find ourselves visiting someone who is caught in the depths of poverty or comforting one who has just suffered a loss. Do we know how to speak in those situations? Will we be prepared to listen to their stories long enough to hear their needs? Not only is it important for us to consider the context of our witnessing encounter, but to understand the matter of receptivity to the gospel as well.

RECEPTIVITY AND LISTENING

Jack Smith has identified within the parable of the soils different levels of receptivity to the gospel. He defines receptivity as "an aptness to receive ideas; being open to and responsive to ideas, impressions and suggestions. Receptivity to the gospel is made up of attitudes which are sometimes affected by the depth of understanding of the gospel."[5] There is little way for us to comprehend the level of understanding of the gospel that Smith speaks about unless we are willing to listen to people in the context of their receptivity to it.

A person characterized as #1 is a "good soil" person. He is spiritually needy, often convicted of sin already, feels guilty, and is searching. He knows he is lost, believes in judgment, and understands the jargon and concepts underlying the gospel. This person will typically come to religious services and enjoys the fellowship of Christians. He will usually receive the witness, trust him, and will often be of a humble spirit when the gospel is presented.

A person characterized as #2 is a "rocky soil person." She often feels justified by her works. She may feel guilty, but knows that she is not really that bad. She will often compare herself to others. And she believes that people will be judged by the good they do. She will attend worship services when she feels it will help her earn some points with God. And she sees a distinct separation between the clergy and

---

5. Jack Smith, *Building Witnessing Relationships* (Atlanta: Home Mission Board, SBC).

regular people. She is comfortable with others like her and with Christians who do not rock the boat (they don't bother ever to witness). She really gets uncomfortable around people who are honestly spiritual in their outlook on life.

A person characterized as #3 is a "thorny soil person." He feels saved or lost based on emotion or on indicators of success or failure in his life. He is goal-oriented and feels that religion is good because it will help him to become more successful, especially in business. He wants to have Jesus in his life, but lordship is another matter. He will attend church if he thinks that it will help to achieve his goals. He believes that some church leaders are credible; he is comfortable with other success-driven people.

A person characterized as #4 is a "hard soil" person. He does not understand the gospel. He really does not need God in his life. I met this person in Las Vegas. He feels self-made. He depends upon science, education, money, you name it, for security. He is usually secular and often a humanist. He will not attend any church service. He thinks the church does some good works, but he does not need it. He believes it is all right for you to follow Christ, but he doesn't think it is right for you to expect him to do so.

Each of these levels of receptivity needs to be understood by the person who would be a caring witness. Dialogue will be different in each situation. The witness will have to listen differently in each situation. Probing questions may be an absolute must for the hard soil person, but quite unnecessary for the good soil person who is ready to receive Jesus.

As you begin to practice the art of listening in order to tell others about your faith in Jesus Christ, pay careful attention to others around you. Begin sizing up others in your mind. Listen carefully to the way they talk. Are they a 1, 2, 3, or 4? Listen to what they are interested in. Who or what is god in their life? Is it self, money, fun, leisure time, work, sex?

Begin dialogue with a good soil person first. Try your best to communicate the gospel in loving, dialogical ways, being careful to ask questions on the level of a 1. Then find a person who seems to be a 2. Notice the need to explore in areas that you did not have to address with a 1. You will probably be discouraged if you try to begin witnessing with a 4. He is a hard case and will require much prayer and direction by the Holy Spirit. He will require hours of dialogue and meaningful conversation. But in any case, respond to the leadership of the Holy Spirit. It may be that the Spirit of God will lead you to a very hard person the first time you try to witness. If this is the case, depend on God's leading. He will instruct you what to say, and He will teach you how to listen to His leading. At the same time, remember to pay attention to people and listen to what they have to say.

THINGS TO THINK ABOUT

1.   EXPLORE THE CONCEPTS.

What kind of emotional baggage do you believe people bring to the witnessing encounter? Make a list. What does each item suggest about how you should deal with the individual exhibiting that particular response?

2.   SEARCH THE SCRIPTURES.

Find as many examples as you can in Scripture that deal with emotional baggage. How was it handled?

3.   DISCUSS THE PRINCIPLES.

Think about how you might be heard by another. How important is your body language? How important is context in the witnessing encounter?

4.   ACT ON WHAT YOU HAVE LEARNED.

Make a list of persons you would like to see trust Jesus as Savior. Then characterize them according to the soils. Plan a strategy to reach them. How will you use dialogue and listening skills?

Chapter 7

CUTTING THROUGH THE FOG

"You must listen to everything he tells you."

Acts 3:22

I am in Moscow, Russia, at the writing of this chapter. Never have I been as lost as I am now, at least in the sense of not knowing how to read street signs, speak the language, or understand much about the culture. I can't order lunch. I realize that if I get sick I could not tell anyone to get me to a doctor—unless somehow they could interpret my hand signals or the pained look on my face. Every time I open my mouth, people look at me and shrug their shoulders. And when they speak to me it sounds like a record being played backwards.

There is nothing wrong with the Russians or with their language. In fact, I am convicted by the fact that so many of them know a little English, yet I know no Russian. It reminds me of just how America-centric most of us are. There is a world out there and we ought to get to know a little more about it! I saw a cartoon recently that spoke to me about this issue. It pictured a huge globe and two young children looking at it with wide eyes and commenting. The caption read, "You know, with the exception of us, the whole world is made up of foreigners." I am afraid that cartoon tells us through humor how prone we are to judging everything through our very subjective point of view.

Anyway, the fog that I feel myself in is very real. The Russian interpreter in the class I am teaching gets confused when I use a Georgia colloquialism. What I think is a funny story often does not translate well. He has to fill in as best as he can and something often gets lost.

President Jimmy Carter once said that he addressed a crowd of persons through a translator. He told a mildly funny story but to his amazement the crowd roared with laughter. He was surprised to find that they thought the story was so funny. Later he asked his interpreter about it. He was told, "Your story was not funny and would not translate into our language. But in our country we would not want to insult you. They laughed because I told them, 'President Carter has just told a funny story; now we must all laugh very loudly.'"

In our nation, where as many as 60 percent are unchurched and possibly as many as one-third of the population are nonreligiously oriented, the problem of communicating the evangel of God can be as frustrating as trying to navigate through a Russian menu when you are starving. And yet, that is precisely the problem we face with evangelism today in America. So many people have overheard the gospel that it makes no real impact on them anymore. Many modern-day pagans, such as many in the baby buster generation who have been raised in a baby boomer home devoid of religious teaching, have no idea who Jesus is. They are in a thick fog of misinformation and misunderstanding. What religious understanding they have is at best only a blur: bits and pieces of New Age, secular humanism, universalism, Americanism, and various other misconceptions.

Donald Posterski has commented that Christianity and North American culture are inseparable.[1] Herein lies one of the major contributors to the fog that witnesses have to cut through. The major problem with Americans, at least as I see it, is that we do not listen very well. We talk a lot; we have lots of opinions; but by and large we don't do a lot of listening. Stop almost any American and he will be an expert on something. She will have an opinion about virtually any topic. That's our nature. Americans are confident people, rugged individualists. That has been our heritage. We are not nearly as reserved as people in other cultures. Travel a little and you will see what I mean.

So, the first layer of fog that we have to learn to cut through is listening like an American—that is, listening while all the time getting ready to offer an opinion about what has just been said, assuming that everyone else in the world is just like mainstream Americans. Even Americans are different, yet we still fall prey to mainstreaming everyone. America is not a "Leave It to Beaver" country anymore. Values have shifted. Americans do not agree on much anymore. Kids carry guns to school. Many parents will not support teachers who try to discipline their children. Children are having children. Drugs gross more money in some states than any other industry. When we listen with our mainstream assumptions, we miss whole segments of the population who

---

1. Donald C. Posterski, *Reinventing Evangelism* (Downers Grove: InterVarsity Press, 1989), 80.

never heard of "the Beaver." And they know nothing of an America where religious values used to be the bedrock that most people accepted.

A second layer of fog includes the element of Americanism. It is the Anglo-American worldview. White people are becoming a minority. America is fast becoming multicolored—not just black, not just white, but yellow, brown, and every other skin color under the sun. We are becoming a nation that is a microcosm of the world in terms of ethnicity. Already, among Southern Baptists, some of the fastest growing churches are ethnic. If it were not for our ethnic work each year, our baptisms would be even lower than they presently are. Ethnics baptize more people than Anglos. They also do a better job of networking within their culture in terms of the gospel than Anglos.

Yet, we often communicate the gospel using Anglo language. This fact was driven home to me in Russia. I was teaching witnessing techniques to my class of Russian students. I made the comment that the Home Mission Board of the SBC printed a tract once for use in restaurants. It was called "A Tip for a V.I.P." The tract was designed so the customer could slip a dollar or two into the tract and leave the gratuity on the table with the tract around it. It is perfectly normal for people in the U.S. who eat in restaurants to tip. And generally, more white business people, eat in restaurants than any other group. You don't see too many poor people eating in nice restaurants, let alone tipping. So, for a moment I forgot where I was and used the illustration about tipping.

The class roared with laughter. I realized what had happened even before the translator told me. The average Russian doesn't have enough money to eat in restaurants, to say nothing of tipping. It was an Anglo-American illustration. If we are not careful we can be guilty of communicating white, Anglo middle-class religion rather than the gospel. A lot of success religion that is being preached today is guilty in this regard: trust God and grow rich. The reality is that many poor minorities in this nation will never grow rich, whether people from that ethnic group trust God or not. Our society has not ridded itself of racism; it is alive and well today. We still have ways to be racist. And a new racism is emerging among many in the baby buster group as they seek to grab all they can.

Charles Kraft has identified scientific humanism as another problem.[2] Science has become our new-found faith as Americans. Since Americans have tended to believe that ignorance is the original sin, the way to perfection is education. People now believe that the way to beat AIDS is through education in matters of safe sex. Abstinence is not the answer; that's too old fashioned they believe. Many believe it is ignorant to consider homosexuality a sin; it is just another lifestyle. People must be educated to be more tolerant and afford equal rights to those who choose that lifestyle. Never mind what the Bible teaches about homosexuality (1 Cor. 6:9; 1 Tim. 1:10).

Scientific humanism is one of the thickest blankets of fog that the witness will encounter. The baby buster generation has been raised up in schools devoid of prayer times that were commonplace for the baby boomer generation. They have watched groups like the A.C.L.U. help cast every vestige of religion out of the schools, civic arenas, football games, and graduation ceremonies. And they have watched Christians roll over and play dead. They have not seen Christians assert their rights to exercise their religion, as guaranteed by the Constitution.

In the place of religion in the schools the baby-buster generation has watched science be raised to a god-like status.

2. Charles H. Kraft, *Communication Theory for Church's Witness* (Maryknoll: ORBIS Books, 1991), 164.

Kraft has said that Americans are now "secular and natural-
istic to the core. Religion is seen as private, personal, and irrelevant."[3] The person who wishes to witness to baby busters
today will need to overcome this layer of fog. He will have
to listen carefully to the mindset of this generation, understand it, prepare a defense of the gospel, and present that defense in meaningful dialogue.

Another significant challenge to overcome is the drive
for affluence. America has been used to affluence since the
end of World War II. Prior to the war most of America was
involved in agriculture. The majority of Americans knew of
the simple life that farming afforded. But after the war,
America started moving to the cities, working in factories,
and enjoying a standard of living that outpaced the world.

Recently, I spoke to my father on this very subject. We
talked about the fact that his generation saw the rapid in-
crease in affluence in America, while my generation is
watching America lose its affluence. After the war, my father went to work for the telephone company. He began
climbing poles and installing phones in homes that had never
owned one. As the years passed his job afforded him promo-
tions, and with each came a raise in pay. He was able to own
three different homes, each one nicer and larger than the other. Through the years of raising his family, he bought auto-
mobiles, paid for his home, took vacations, saved money,
invested in stocks with his company, had his health benefits
provided, put two children through college, and retired on a
full pension with health benefits. And he did all of that on a
modest, middle-class salary.

My generation is so different. I have watched America
become a debtor nation. My peers struggle to buy a home of
any size. We work two and one half jobs to keep our standard
of living from deteriorating. Our wives work. Our children

---

3. Kraft, *Communication*, 164.

work. College costs have put our children at risk of being unable to go. We live from day to day never knowing if our jobs are going to be shipped to another country where labor is cheaper. Our health benefits now cost more than our home mortgages. Cars cost more than my father's first home. And all this is taking place as we are making as much as three times what our parents made each year.

Americans are working longer hours and sacrificing more to have less and less. Yet, we still strive for affluence, because we have been raised expecting to be affluent. It is coming as quite a shock to many baby boomers that they will not retire at the same level of affluence as their parents. It is also a concern because many of the 76 million boomers are realizing that they may not even see their children be able to live as they have lived.

America is losing its affluence, even though we are still rich beyond compare to most any other nation. The striving for affluence, however, will often cause people to turn a deaf ear to matters of religion. Career has become the god of many boomers. Cutting through the fog of upward mobility, keeping up with the Jones, and striving for a level of affluence equal to their parents will take time and attention away from many who would otherwise be open to explore matters of faith. The carefully listening evangelist will need to grapple with the disappointments, frustrations, expectations, and goals of this generation if the gospel is to offer them anything they can grasp.

Poverty is another blanket of fog that will need to be cut through. While millions are striving to achieve a level of affluence, millions more are trapped in poverty. There are now more children, women with children, and old people in poverty in this nation than ever before. The decade of the eighties, when government focused on giving advantage to the rich in the form of trickle-down economics, insider stock trading, corporate takeovers, and Reaganomics only served to widen the gap between the haves and the have-nots. The nation's debt grew to gigantic proportions during this era of money grabbing. As a result the nation now is facing an enormous crisis with regard to paying off its debts. People have lost jobs. Social programs have suffered. Homelessness is an epidemic in America today. It is not unusual to see people of all ages alongside the road with hand-lettered signs that read, "I will work for food."

How do you share the gospel with these people? What would Christ say about the church buildings we go into debt to build, the fine carpets, elaborate decor, mega-buck media productions, and soft pews we fashion for ourselves, all in the name of worship? How much money do we spend keeping up the infrastructures of religion and how much do we spend feeding, clothing, and housing people and making it possible for them to hear the gospel above the clamor of hunger in empty stomachs?

Leonardo Boff has reminded us that Jesus' option for the poor means a protest against poverty and an exaltation of the eminent worth and dignity of the person of the poor.[4] But how much money do we spend in defense of the poor? When was the last time you heard of a church willing to forego its own agenda so that poverty could be erased in its community? We must listen to the needs of the poor. When we ask them, they will tell us what these needs are. "An evangelization that does not directly involve the poor, and confirm their hope in a new, different society, an evangelization that does not take up the cause of the poor, their struggles and their lives, loses its Christian destiny, and betrays the historical Jesus, who was a poor person in this world, and who identified with the poor."[5]

---

4. Leonardo Boff, New Evangelization: *Good News to the Poor* (Mary Knoll: ORBIS Books, 1990), 78.
5. Ibid.

Entertainment is a thick fog that has blanketed America today. We spend billions of dollars each year entertaining ourselves, both inside and outside of church. It is amazing to see how our craving for bigger and more elaborate productions in worship has caused even the smallest churches to spend large amounts of money bringing in singing groups, drama teams, building handbell choirs, and orchestras, and the list could go on. Churches now compete to see which can put on the most elaborate program in the community. Recent studies of the popular church growth movement have indicated that many churches have grown, not due to conversion growth, but because they could put on a better program. And smaller churches in the communities have died as members left to go to the more exciting mega-church.

"It has been said that baby boomers do not want to be a part of a church that is not exciting. So many churches have turned to doing whatever attracts a crowd."

A church I know of in a large city has taken so many members away from adjacent churches that even a few previously strong churches have now lost so many members that they are facing serious financial problems. It has been said that baby boomers do not want to be a part of a church that is not exciting. So many churches have turned to doing whatever attracts a crowd.

It used to be that conservative churches did not applaud in the worship services. Now it is commonplace. Applause in itself is not a sin, of course. But to many worshipers, applause smacks of appreciation for worldly entertainment and seems somehow out of place in worship.

In a society where sports heroes make multi-millions of dollars and seem to be the new messiahs, the Christian witness might believe that this entertainment-crazed generation will not entertain a serious thought about its need for salvation.

But we have seen heroes falling from their pedestals. AIDS, scandals, and shortened careers due to drug overdose and other problems have caused many fans to take another look. It is precisely at this point that the Christian witness has an opportunity to share faith.

The church needs to grapple with the issue of entertainment. It needs to offer what the world can never offer. It should not feel it has to become like the world to get people to listen. That is precisely what turns many off; they do not see the church as any different from society. People are looking for something that is real, not tinsel, not Hollywood.

There are other issues that cloud opportunities for witnessing. The listening evangelist must learn to cut through the fog and go to the heart of the issue. Caught in each underlying problem is a person with needs. Our task is to find out about that need and meet it headlong with the good news of Jesus Christ. Learn to identify those things in people's lives that keep them lost in a fog. Don't ignore them, but don't cave in to them either. Understand that sharing the gospel today is far more complex than in any past generation. More things compete for the heart, mind, and money of society. But we also find new opportunities for witness as people discover how empty life can be without Christ. Learn to develop a listening heart.

THINGS TO THINKS ABOUT

1. EXPLORE THE CONCEPTS.

How western is your thinking? America is a country of many languages and cultures. What do the cultural shifts, language patterns, and social changes imply for the way we present the gospel?

2. SEARCH THE SCRIPTURES.

Examine cross-cultural and language barriers that were crossed in the Scriptures. How did Peter talk to Cornelius, for example? What might we learn from this encounter?

3. DISCUSS THE PRINCIPLES.

Discuss in a small group or with a friend the language we use, the customs we reflect, and our presuppositions about how the gospel is received by others. Are there strengths or weaknesses in the way we approach others who may not have the same religious, language, or cultural pre-suppositions as we?

4. ACT ON WHAT YOU HAVE LEARNED.

Develop a friendship with a person from a third world country. Get to know how she thinks, how she sees the world. Dialogue about your faith and her faith. Listen closely to the cultural baggage that your new friend brings to the conversation.

Chapter 8

THE LISTENING HEART

He who answers a matter before he hears it,
it is a folly and shame unto him.

Proverbs 18:13

If you assume you know the answer before you hear the question, you are guilty of folly. We often assume that listening is easy. It takes no effort, or so we think. Just because I have ears doesn't mean I know anything about how to listen. Listening is stressful. It takes enormous concentration. And it is a developed art.

LISTENING IN MY LIFE

I want to tell you a story about my experience with listening. And just because it happened to me this way doesn't make me a perpetual expert at the art of listening. I often have to relearn some of the lessons God wants to teach me every day about how to listen to Him.

Throughout my academic days at The Baptist Theological Seminary, I had a deep-down feeling that I belonged there—not just as a student, but in other ways, ways I could not describe. Maybe it was the tall spires that stood elegantly against the moonlight. Maybe it was my love for my professors or the sense of community I felt at seminary. Whatever it was, I felt it deeply. I often imagined myself teaching there.

When I graduated in 1974, I went to work at the Baptist Sunday School Board in Nashville, Tennessee, as a curriculum editor. Then after five years I was invited to the staff of the Southern Baptist Home Mission Board in Atlanta, where I remained until 1991.

In 1990 I began to sense that God was doing something in my life. I had concurrently served in eight different churches as interim pastor over a period of about seven years. I was very happy in my job as editor of the evangelism section of the HMB and had no wish to make another career move.

However, God began to stir my heart. The problem was that I had no idea why. I was asked to take a series of tests in 1990 to examine my skills and to enhance my potential for other positions of leadership at the HMB. I took four different kinds of exams and then waited to see the results.

When the tests came in, they showed overwhelmingly that my greatest potential lay in teaching. In fact, one of the tests categorized my future potential as that of a professor. I knew that I loved teaching, but had never thought that I would do so.

I brushed off the idea since I really did not believe it would come to pass. I told my wife about the experience and she and I began to talk about how nice it would be to relocate to another state and work in a different field, to let the kids see another part of America. Pipe dreams, or so I thought.

But God had a plan for my life. Seventeen years after I graduated from seminary the dream of my lifetime came true for me. I received a call one day and the provost of the seminary asked me if I would be open to talking to him about teaching. I was overwhelmed. I thought he had the wrong person in mind.

Although I had secretly fantasized about being a professor at my alma mater, I never thought in a million years it would happen. But it did—out of the blue, or so it seemed.

As my wife and I prayed about the decision, it seemed so right at the time. The career tests, my own feeling that God was doing something in my life, and my wife's feeling that God was about to do something all came together around the phone call.

Fully a year before my invitation to teach, my wife had thought about maybe making a move from the ministry where we served to some other field. We even talked about it at dinner one evening with the kids. So when the invitation came from Southern, we knew it was right. We decided to sell our home and move. I went ahead to Southern and left my wife and kids behind to sell the house, confident that God was about to bless us with our heart's desire.

But the housing market dried up at about the time we accepted the new position at the seminary. It seemed that every house in our neighborhood was suddenly on the market. And no one wanted any of them. A year and a half later, my wife and I were still apart. I was seeing my family once a month and we were hurting from the separation. We tried to write letters, talk on the phone, and see one another as often as possible.

It looked like I had made a terrible mistake and had not heard the call of God as I thought I had. What confused me was that I had not initiated the invitation for me to go to Southern. It seemed that God had worked it out. And I loved teaching. Yet our house did not sell.

Nearly two years went by. My wife prayed. She heard God say very clearly to her that we should not move. The fact that the house did not sell, along with some other factors, seemed to reinforce her conviction that we should not make a permanent move to Louisville. I could not understand. I prayed and the heavens seemed silent. God had blessed my teaching ministry. All was going well with my teaching and with the students. The only negative was that my family was not with me.

I decided to stick it out until I knew an answer from God. I just prayed and prayed. I don't know how many times I prayed for God to sell our house and get our family together so I could carry on with my teaching. Yet all the while my wife was telling me that she felt God did not want us to make the move permanently.

It seemed like gridlock. I was caught between God's call, my wife's understanding of God's will, a house that would not sell, and no job if I just quit and went back home. What was God up to? How could my wife and I hear God in different ways? I don't mind telling you that it was a scary set of circumstances. Never before in my life had I ever faced such confusion.

I determined to keep on praying—praying for God to sell our home, to get our family back together, to salvage my ministry in Louisville.

One day I got a telephone call from a friend of mine. Nell called to see how I was. We had known one another in Atlanta and she had recently moved to Louisville. I told her of the situation and she asked me to come pray with her about it. Nell is the kind of prayer warrior that can get on her knees and reach right into the throne room of heaven.

So we both got on our knees and I began to pray. I prayed my usual prayer. "God help me sell my house, get my family back together, and carry on with our ministry here in Louisville." Then Nell began to pray. And she prayed. And she wept. And in the middle of her praying, she turned to me and said, "Ron, maybe God doesn't intend to sell your house. Maybe He doesn't want you here for a lifetime."

I felt like a mountain fell on top of me. I love and respect Nell and did not want to tell her how mistaken I thought she was. After all, God had called me to teach. My wife and I knew it. What we did not understand was why things were not working out. And why my wife was now having second thoughts.

I went back to my apartment and got on my knees and prayed some more. And I wept. That weekend I went home and my wife and I talked some more about the situation. The day before I was due to drive back to Louisville, God answered our prayers in a dramatic way.

My wife and I had agreed that we needed a clear sign from God to help us see His will more clearly. So we prayed and told God that we would respond to what He showed us. And God provided that sign for us. There was no mistake about it. I knew then that God had a plan. And that I had been so busy telling God what He had to do to keep my ministry in Louisville in tact that I could not hear Him saying what my wife had heard, what Nell had heard, and what He wanted to tell me: "I do not want you here teaching for a career, but just a little while." This was the furthest thing from my mind. It made no sense until I stopped talking and finally listened to God.

I determined that I would go back to Louisville, teach through the end of the year and then resign. I had no idea what I would do, but for the first time in more than a year and a half, I was at peace. I had finally heard God. I was no longer afraid of the future. The next two months I determined to pray differently. I began to pray, "Lord, help me listen to you. Tell me what you want me to do next, and I will do it."

Within two months, God did clearly tell us what He wanted my wife and me to do in our ministry. Again, out of the blue, or so I thought, I received a call. This time it was from a place that I would not have considered as a ministry position in a million years. I was invited to become the director of evangelism for my home state of Georgia. The search committee told me that they had been praying for months for the right person and that they had been led of God to me. They were waiting upon God. And God was waiting for me to listen to His instructions. The two years I spent teaching actually prepared me for the position I now hold in the Georgia Baptist Convention. And the new ministry position did not require me to move nor sell my home.

Had I been mistaken about my call to teach? Absolutely not. But it took two years for God to equip me with the additional credentials I needed for my new position, two years for me to make a contribution that was needed at Southern, and two years for me to listen to God and find out that His plan was entirely different from my agenda.

Perhaps in your experience you have had an occasion when the heavens have seemed silent. When that happens, tell God that you are going to stop telling Him what you want. Tell Him you are going to listen. More than likely, when you really get silent and listen, He will reveal what He wants you to know.

When you and I learn to listen to God, to others, to our wives, to our husbands or best friends, to the lost, there are some important things to remember. One of the most important is to learn to deal with the many barriers to listening.

SELECTIVE LISTENING

All of us listen selectively. If we didn't we'd go crazy. Without our ability to listen selectively, all the noise around us would put us into a nervous frenzy. The air conditioner is running next to me here in my study. It is Saturday morning and my wife is running the vacuum in the next room. The keyboard I am typing on is going clicky clack. My stomach is growling because I am hungry, and now and then our little wirehair terrier barks at a cat outside. But in spite of all those sounds (the phone just rang!), I am listening to my thoughts. As best as I can do it, I have selected to listen to my thoughts rather than the air conditioner and all the other sounds in the room.

When we selectively listen to another person the results can be either positive or negative. It can be positive when we listen for emotions or agenda that are underneath the words that someone is speaking. In doing this, we can often get a better idea about the hurt they are dealing with or the issue that is really at the root of their response.

Selective listening becomes negative when we adopt the attitude, "I told you so." When we listen to someone and yet listen for what we want to hear based on our preconceived notions or opinions, we are guilty of negative listening. Have you ever heard someone make a speech during a political rally, for example? One person may come away inspired and another very negative. What is the difference? It is all in what we listen for.

PREJUDICE

Prejudice is a danger to the listening heart. When we make up our minds that the person is a drunk, for example, and will always be one, we will not react to that person with sensitivity to what made him an alcoholic. Or when a person's skin color is different from ours, what they say may be heard in terms of our attitudes toward that race.

Last year a popular film came out with the title *White Men Can't Jump*. It was a story about basketball, but the title betrays a certain racism. Are all whites unable to jump? Are all blacks lazy or on public assistance? Are all Mexicans illegal aliens? Are all who live in the South sluggish in their speech and all who live in the North short tempered and rude?

Prejudice affects us all. We have to constantly work to keep ourselves from listening to others through filters of prejudice. If a person has a bad reputation, does that mean he cannot be saved? A pastor friend told me of an incident that happened in his church.

The opportunity came to the church to offer an evangelistic ministry to those who attended automobile races at a popular racetrack each weekend. When the idea was being discussed someone commented that the people who attended those races were just beer-guzzling rednecks. They would not care to hear the gospel.

But when that comment was made, someone else in the group answered, "Yes, they may be beer-drinkers and some may act like rednecks, but all of them are people for whom Jesus died." Prejudice will kill evangelistic efforts and can turn our ears off to the needs of people.

POINT OF VIEW BLINDNESS

Point of view blindness can best be illustrated by observing the old saying that everyone looks at the world through his own knothole. Harvey Robbins tells a story to illustrate this problem.

"You've heard the story of the young boy who, after watching a baseball game, walked up to the three umpires and asked them how they call balls and strikes. The first umpire said, "Well, some's balls and some's strikes, and I calls 'em as I sees 'em." The second umpire said, "Well, some's balls and some's strikes, and I calls 'em as they are." The third umpire said, "Well, some's balls and some's strikes, but they ain't nothin' til I calls 'em."[1]

Five Barriers That Keep Us From Listening Well

1. **Selective listening**
2. **Prejudice**
3. **Point of view blindness**
4. **Mistaken motives**
5. **Hasty conclusions**

No other person is like you. No other person is like me. All of us view the world through our own experiences. In many ways we have to try to get outside of ourselves when we really want to listen to another person. As much as possible we have to try to put ourselves in her shoes. What does she feel about her life? How did she grow up?

We may smile and say God is a wonderful Heavenly Father to a lost person. But we might not realize that as a child that person's father beat her or abused her sexually. She may have grown up with the worst kind of image of what a father ought to be. If we do not take time to listen to the person, how will we ever know? Don't assume that everyone has had a life exprcience like yours, good or bad.

---

1. Harvey A. Robbins, *How to Speak and Listen Effectively* (New York: AMA-COM Press, 1992), 13–14.

I have heard personal testimonies that almost seemed to glorify the wicked life the person used to lead. Sometimes the person will go into great detail about his former life, hoping to paint a sharp contrast between the way he used to live and how he lives since becoming a Christian. Sometimes it is effective. Other times it leaves the audience thinking he had a better time as a lost person. In most of those cases, I cannot identify at all with the speaker. I was brought up in a loving, Christ-honoring home. All of my life I have been in church. Even my "rebellious years" were tame compared to some stories I have heard. I was saved at the age of ten, and I thank God for that fact. It would be a mistake to think that others have had the same kind of experiences that I have had.

We need to look through the other person's knothole, view the world as she does. You might even find this new viewpoint interesting.

MISTAKEN MOTIVES

Mistaken motives also can hinder our listening. Have you ever found yourself pre-judging a situation or a person? Have you ever been critical of a person's motive, only to find out later that you were wrong in your judgment of that motive?

Over twenty years ago, while I was in college, I worked at a city newspaper. Our paper did quite well and was recognized for its outstanding journalism. My weekly sports section was awarded a prize for excellence, and as a result I was invited to attend the state press association meeting.

The meeting was marked by dinners, speeches, and entertainment. I went with a colleague from another paper in a sister city. The cold war was on and most people did not look with favor on anyone from the Soviet Union. That evening's after-dinner speaker, however, was a Communist official from Moscow. The text of his speech sought to show the advantages of communism over capitalism and to illustrate how much better life was in the Soviet Union.

My friend next to me was visibly shaken. Several times during the speech he leaned over to me and whispered strong negative comments about the speaker. He could not fathom why this person would have been invited to address such a distinguished crowd of newspaper publishers and writers. He squirmed in his seat and would not even look at the speaker. He was miserable.

About five minutes into the speech, though, I began to notice that the speaker's accent was a little phony. And then came the puns. I remember one very clearly. He said to the crowd there, "You have freedom to own land in the United States. That's not so special. We own land in Russia also. Six by six by three." The crowd roared with laughter. My friend grumbled. He failed to see the humor in the comment.

As the speech continued, it became more and more obvious. This guy was an entertainer. He had used the phony Communist uniform and accent as a part of his act. As it turned, out he was a show business entertainer from Missouri! I had sore sides from laughing so hard.

My friend went away miserable and depressed. He had totally misread the motives of the entertainer. His motives were not to convince us that the Communist form of government was better than democracy. His motive was to entertain. And he did it in a unique fashion. There is danger in misreading motives. When you listen to someone, give the conversation time. You may be turned off at first. But as you go deeper into the conversation you might find that you have mistaken the person's motive for what he said.

HASTY CONCLUSIONS

Haste makes waste. How many times have we heard that said? And yet it is true, and the same principle applies to the listening heart. When we jump to conclusions about another person based on selective listening, prejudice, point of view blindness, or mistaken motives, the result is a hasty conclusion, and often a faulty one.

Leading a person to faith in Jesus Christ is not a snap. Sometimes we think that a five-minute presentation and a two-minute prayer is all it takes with every person we meet. God can save a person in the twinkle of an eye if He chooses, although it may take a period of years.

The witnessing process is hurt when we rush in and do not give the person we are talking to the time she needs to react, to ask questions, to clarify understandings of the gospel, or to seek directions about living the new life in Christ. The gospel message, while simple enough for a child to grasp, has tremendous implications for living. These implications are not often easy to grasp all at once. In fact, most Christians spend a lifetime trying to grasp the implications of truly living the Christ life. Every moment spent in prayer, every verse studied in God's word, every witnessing encounter brings new insight and correctives or additions to our knowledge of God.

The listening heart of the witness will avoid hasty conclusions that imply another has fully grasped the gospel. Rather, the caring witness will ask questions, help to clarify concepts, give the person time to digest the implications of a new life in Christ, and walk through the journey with the person through meaningful dialogue. Ask God to give you a listening heart.

THINGS TO THINK ABOUT

1.   EXPLORE THE CONCEPTS.

Think about your life story or some portion of it. Has there ever been an occasion when your heart listened differently from everyday life patterns? If so, write it out and analyze it. Reflect on what you learned.

2.   SEARCH THE SCRIPTURES.

Find passages or stories in the Scripture when persons learned new things from time spent with God. What new things could you learn?

3.   DISCUSS THE PRINCIPLES.

Discuss with your group or with a friend the barriers that keep us from listening well. Determine ways to correct the problem in your life.

4.   ACT ON WHAT YOU HAVE LEARNED.

Keep a journal for a week. Write a paragraph describing a situation that made you listen selectively, that caused prejudice to surface, etc. How could the situation be different?

Chapter 9

GIVING A REDEMPTIVE WORD

*Whoever knows God listens to us; but whoever is not
from God does not listen to us.*

1 John 4:6

Now that you have learned the importance of listening
and hopefully have some additional insights into listening,
how do you tell someone about Jesus? How do you verbalize
the gospel in the midst of listening and dialogue? We have
seen that no rigid set of rules can be laid down that will work
all the time. That is precisely what is wrong with using a rigid
gospel presentation for every occasion regardless of context or
situation. God is sovereign in His work and never deals with

any two people in exactly the same way. For this reason the witness must lean heavily upon God for direction, listen to the leadership of the Holy Spirit, and by all means listen to the person He is talking to. However, as you are giving a redemptive witness try to approach the process using the following tips. Remember to observe the lost person carefully and determine his orientation to religious concepts. Some will be very clear and understand much of what you're saying. Others will be less clear.

TIP NO. 1:
COMMUNICATE GENUINE INTEREST

In conversation with a lost person, do your best to communicate genuine interest in the other person and communicate your personal sense of her value before God. The way you show interest in her life story, the eye contact you make, and the affirmation you give that she has something worthwhile to say all go a long way toward communicating genuine interest. George Hunter, Jr. has said of secular people that the message we need to communicate to them is that they matter to God.[1] So don't be in too much of a hurry to talk. Let her tell her life story. Encourage her to empty her soul. Bill Gordon tells of a woman who was very hostile to the gospel. She attacked with venom the person who wanted to tell her about Jesus. The wise witness simply responded, "Would you mind just telling me who hurt you and the circumstances that led to that hurt?" For the next hour she emptied herself of the venom in her life and her rejection of all things spiritual. He patiently sat and listened and then was able to tell her about Jesus with less resistance.[2]

---

1. From a lecture given at the Academy for Theological Education in Evangelism annual meeting, Lancaster, Pa., 1992.
2. Interview with Bill Gordon.

Don't put a stopwatch on the witnessing event. Most people will need help in telling their own story, so don't be afraid to ask questions, to direct gently the conversation, affirm, or ask for clarification. As you develop the dialogue, begin to ask questions of a deeper nature, such as, "Have you ever thought about why you are here on this earth?" or "What kind of legacy do you want to leave when people remember your life?" Gently move them to a place where they will begin to open up avenues to a discussion of what they believe about God, about life after death, or salvation. Don't argue, just listen.

TIP NO. 2:
COMMENT ON THE PERSON'S LIFE STORY

A second tip in giving a redemptive witness is to comment on the person's life story. For example, you might find a very interesting point in the life story and comment on it. "I never realized that you had training as a nurse. I have always known you as a reporter for our town's newspaper. How did you get from nursing to reporting the news?" This process shows that you are genuinely interested in the other person and that you really are listening. Try to help the person realize their enormous potential in life. Then direct them in a discussion about their giftedness and about God who is the giver of gifts to men and women, as well as life itself. Be creative and build on opportunities presented by the person's life story. Remember, when you are dealing with a person who has little or no religious orientation to life, it is vital to connect his life to God's desire for him to have a full and meaningful life. Since he has probably never considered this before, spend some time helping him to explore God's concern for his life and reinforce that Jesus came to die for him because his life matters to God.

Tip No. 3:
Explore a Religious Concept Together

Explore a religious concept and ask the person to comment on it in terms of his life story. Briefly comment on a spiritual concept and ask the person if they agree or would like to add anything from their insight to your observations. For example, "I have always felt as a Christian that God gave leadership to my life." "Have you ever felt that God wanted to direct your life?" Then listen for the feedback to occur. If you are witnessing to a cult member, understand that these people are religiously oriented. They enjoy talking about spiritual things. Don't let the fact that they are in a cult or in the New Age movement keep you from talking in general ways about spiritual things, even though you may hear some strange things being said to you. Instead, listen. Then respond and focus your remarks toward the gospel. Don't feel that you have to present all the tenets of the faith as a response at one time. Rather deal with an issue at a time. Understand that you are planting seed. You are not harvesting yet. The harvest can come later; it will take some time.

Tip No. 4:
Reinforce Your Visit

During the week do something tangible to reinforce to the person that you heard their life story. If they are interested in history, for example, buy them a book on some aspect of history. Give the book as a gift along with a note of appreciation for the conversation you had and a note of encouragement to get together again for further conversation. Try to use a note that has an inspirational verse on it, or write your own verse on the bottom of the note. Be aware if you are communicating with a person from another culture that a gift may make them feel obligated to you. Do not put them into an uncomfortable position. Be aware of any symbolic meanings that a gift might convey. Decide upon an action to take that would reinforce the importance of your time together, and use that action to convey a redemptive word of witness.

TIP NO. 5:
KEEP IT SIMPLE

When you discuss religious concepts, remember to keep the discussion simple. Get to know the level of theological understanding of the person you are talking with. Watch his eyes. Watch for facial expressions when you talk about religious concepts. If the person lacks a strong religious orientation to life, be careful not to use theological buzz words like justification, sanctification, or even redemption. Even for someone who was raised in a Christian environment but has never made a decision to trust Christ as Savior and Lord, some terms may be difficult to comprehend. Instead tell the story of Jesus' life and His death on the cross in as simple detail as you can. Later on in the discipleship process with the person, greater depth can be attained as you discuss the implications of salvation for his life. Try as often as you can to connect the implications for salvation to your own life story. You will never be able to convince most people through argument, but they cannot dispute what you say has happened to you spiritually. They might not understand it, but they cannot deny it. Don't complicate; rather take time to explain in simple English what it means to confess your sins, to ask God to forgive sins, to receive Jesus as Lord, and so on. Give as many illustrations from your life as you believe will be helpful. Remember, some people with whom you talk have no idea who Jesus is and are totally unaware of the process of salvation, so explain carefully. Followup with questions: "Does this make any sense to you?" "What did you just hear me say?" Then listen.

Tip No. 6:
Test the Person's Readiness to Go Further

Test the person's readiness to go further. If they are ready to go further, use the Bible to show them what Jesus demands of us in salvation. Use a version of the Bible such as the *New American Standard Bible* or another version that helps simplify concepts. Remember that some people know the Bible as the title of a book, not as the Word of God. At this point, do not be afraid to point out the Scriptures that talk about salvation, man's sinfulness, and his need of a Savior. Do this especially if you determine that the person is understanding religious concepts or is religiously oriented. Use Scripture verses you may have learned in witnessing classes, such as those in CWT or EE, and others as a guide such as those found in Romans (the Roman Road). Ask the person to comment on what you have read. Listen to him comment. Ask him if he has questions. Ask him to paraphrase the concepts you have discussed. Talk about the concepts in Scripture. Help him to put into his own words what the Scriptures say. Listen to his response. Be prepared to explain concepts if the person is unclear about anything you have said..

"Don't put a stopwatch on the witnessing event."

Tip No. 7:
Recognize Those Who Are Ready

Understand that some people are ready for harvesting. If you find a person who has told you of his readiness to receive Jesus, realize that this person is a category #1 or good soil person. As you present the gospel to the person, use talk-back. Ask her if she understands. It is here that you can use a more deductive approach to the witnessing process. Don't be afraid of it. Use it, but listen all the while and observe the other person to see if anything is going over her head, or if she is more into the systematized plan or presentation than into the concepts you are trying to get her to understand. Stop often and listen to her.

TIP NO. 8:
LISTEN

Remind yourself of the importance of silence in the encounter. After a person has told his or her life story, or after you have begun to discuss the gospel, pause for a time and ask the person to think about what you have just been talking about. Then wait. Let them pick up the conversation again, if possible. Or suggest that you both get a soft drink and that you spend a few minutes going over the concepts privately. Allow appropriate time for silence and then let the other person take the lead in getting the dialogue moving again. In these moments of silence, the Holy Spirit can water and fertilize the comments you have made about salvation. He can drive home the Scripture you have read, and the other person can assimilate some of what he has heard in terms of his practical experience.

Remember what Henri Nouwen has said: "We have become so contaminated by our wordy world that we hold to the deceptive opinion that our words are more important than our silence."[3] Your task is to help the lost person become aware of the movement of God in his heart. He is like a person in the dark of night looking for something that is lost.

---

3. Henri J. M. Nouwen, *The Way of the Heart* (San Francisco: Harper Press, 1981), 58.

You are providing him a light and the Holy Spirit is directing him toward Jesus. Every comment, every moment of silence shines on new ground. For the lost person this is a new experience. He needs time to assimilate it.

Encourage him by speaking a word that anticipates what God is doing in his heart. Say to him, for example, "John, as we have talked you may be feeling some sense of urgency to respond, but maybe you still have many questions. Why don't you just pause right now and ask God to answer just one of your questions?" Then give the process time for God to speak to John. Encourage him to reflect. Ask John, after a time, to tell you what he heard God saying. Out of the times of silence that you allow for in the witnessing process, God may redirect the encounter in ways that meet the lost person's need that you would not have discovered had you not allowed some time for silence and reflection.

No doubt other tips will come to you as you reflect on ways to integrate dialogue, silence, and sensitivity toward people as you are sharing the gospel. Once you are in the process of sharing the gospel and giving a redemptive response to someone whom you know needs to be saved or who is seeking to know God, the next step involved is that of handling their response.

THINGS TO THINK ABOUT

1. EXPLORE THE CONCEPTS.

Review the tips given for sharing a word of witness. Explore each tip and let your mind think of examples, situations, or creative ideas to enhance the tips given in the chapter.

2. SEARCH THE SCRIPTURES.

Go through the Scriptures and find examples to support each of the tips given. For example, tip number three was a part of the woman at the well story. She explored a religious concept with Jesus. Nicodemus also talked about a religious concept that Jesus commented on. Find others.

3. DISCUSS THE PRINCIPLES.

In your small group, discuss thoroughly each of the tips. Share a witnessing situation you are currently involved in. Ask the group to help you determine which tip would work best in the situation. Be sure to report back to the group.

4. ACT ON WHAT YOU HAVE LEARNED.

Determine this week to carry out at least one tip mentioned in the chapter. Remember, what you learn will be just an academic exercise unless it is put into action.

Chapter 10

HANDLING RESPONSE

And all the people listened attentively.

Nehemiah 8:3

As you share with people in this inductive ministry of listening to tell, response will come in a variety of ways. You must know how to handle the kinds of response that you will face.

Not all of the responses will be positive. That is the risk you take everytime you witness. But remember, your job as a witness is to plant the seed. Planting seeds of witness in a life should be a joyful experience. If you also have the opportunity to harvest the seed that may have been planted earlier in the life of a person, that too will be a joyful experience.

CORNELIUS

The first response could be called the *Cornelius model*. There are persons who have been just looking for someone to come along and clarify their searching. They are usually religiously sensitive and seeking. With this person all you generally have to do is to approach them with the gospel and they will respond with positive affirmation.

Recently, I was eating at a restaurant and the waitress who served me did so with unusual kindness. At the end of my meal she served me with my bill and said that it was a pleasure to serve me. Then she walked away to her station and stood quietly. I noticed that she was not busy, so I got out an appropriate gratuity and decided to speak to her about the service and hand her the gratuity in person.

I told her that I was impressed with her kindness. I have eaten at many restaurants in the past and she really stood out as being friendly and helpful. I sensed that she was approachable and was not busy, so I asked her if she was from the area. She indicated that she was new in town. I then asked her if she had a church home. She said that she did not attend church.

I was somewhat surprised but tried not to show it. I decided to redirect the conversation.

"The reason that I asked you about your church membership was that I assumed you might be a Christian, since you showed such kindness to me. Could I ask you if you are a Christian?"

She replied. "No, I am not, but I have always wanted to be. In fact, I was reading my Bible last night trying to find out how to become one."

This lady was ready to hear the gospel. I happened to have a witnessing tract in my pocket and asked her permission to share it. She granted me permission and I briefly led her through the tract. She smiled and gratefully received all I had to say. At the end she was ready to ask Christ into her heart.

Here was a lady who was searching. I came along and showed her how to become a Christian. This was a case where I simply picked the fruit that was ripe. I used a tract, a systematized presentation of the gospel, and that was appropriate in her case. Throughout the presentation we talked about the experience of asking Christ into one's heart. In the small amount of time I had I tried to do everything I could to insure that she understood and that I moved her to the place where she could make the decision she was wanting to make. I gave her my name and number and asked her to call me with any questions. I invited her to my church and hoped she would attend.

This lady apparently had the seed of the gospel presented to her life in times passed. Something had been happening in her life to bring her to Christ. My joy was being there and being able to direct her and simply clarify her questions and her seeking, but not everyone is like this lovely lady.

FELIX

Some people are reserved in their response. There are some people to whom you will present the gospel and with whom you will dialogue who will still reserve the right to decide the matter on their own terms. They will put off the decision to follow Christ. One can identify this person as demonstrating the *Felix model*. "Go away for the present, and when I find time, I will summon you" (Acts 24:25).

They listen to your presentation of the gospel and they discuss the implications for their life, but somehow they cannot bring themselves to the point of real commitment. When this happens, realize that you are at a temporary stopping place. It will do little good to try and push them further. It may even do harm.

I learned this lesson during one of my pastorates. I was asked to go and see a man who lived on the outskirts of town. He was known by many in the congregation as a possible prospect for our church. His children attended the church, but neither he nor his wife did. One of the children had been talking to her father, however, and he had seemed interested in spiritual things. So she came to me and asked me to go and visit him and to try to tell him about Jesus.

I went to the home and spent about an hour talking with him about his life and about his need for Christ. He was very cordial. He never once seemed hostile or unwilling to talk about his need of salvation.

I thought, based on what I had heard, that it was time to ask him for a commitment of his life. But when I asked him if there was any reason that would keep him from asking Christ into his life, he shocked me by saying, "Yes, there is. I am just not ready to do so. I will do it some time later."

I began to warn him that later might not come. I told him a couple of tragic stories of people who had died before they made a decision to invite Christ into their lives. And then I saw anger flare in his eyes. "Look, I told you, not now!" And he turned away from me with indifference. The conversation was over. He never granted me another interview. I had dropped the ball in my zeal to get him to make a decision. I wish now that I had honored his statement, given him a gospel tract to look over or some other helpful evangelistic material to consider, and then left for a later time. He probably would have talked with me further had I not ignored his wish to see me later.

I realize that people can put off the gospel until they die and go into eternity never making the most important decision for eternity. That's the risk we take when we witness. We cannot coerce anyone to accept Jesus when he wants to put it off. We have to try and come back at a later time, or perhaps take a different tact with him. Certainly we need to bathe the situation in prayer and ask God to help us reach the person through careful cultivation.

DOUBTING THOMAS

Then there are those who are like *doubting Thomas*. Sometimes in spite of all you do to explain the gospel, they cannot bring themselves to believe that it is real or that God could ever love them enough to die for them. They need more proof.

For some people the reality of trauma in their emotional lives prohibits them from understanding that they can be loved. You may never uncover this fact in the witnessing conversation. Some who have been physically abused cannot deal with the idea that another can love them. They may hide their history of abuse and not realize that they are not to blame for it. If you suspect that this is the case, or if the conversation leads you to believe the person is dealing with a great deal of emotional pain, you may want to help them meet with a Christian counselor who can guide them through the process of healing. In such a case, do not simply hand them over to another. Walk with them through the process. Demonstrate to them your care and love for them.

There are some who doubt because they have been confused over some point in your discussions. They are not entirely clear about the gospel. Remember, meaning is not ascribed to the words you are saying. Rather, meaning occurs when the other person decodes those words and then attaches his own meaning to the words. He may have misunderstood a concept that is causing him to be cautious or to doubt.

When that happens, go back and help him verbalize the points at which he is confused or about which he has questions. Do not leave the issue until he is able to verbalize his understanding and until you make sure that his understanding is biblical.

Do not be afraid of doubt. Doubt is a healthy negative response. The opposite of love is not hate, it is indifference. Doubt may seem to be a turn-off to the gospel or a negative response. It is not necessarily so. It may be just a signal that something is not clear yet. So when doubt occurs, go back and discover together where the breakdown occurred.

DEMAS

Some are like *Demas*. They love other things. Their commitment is shallow. Shallow commitment is always a disappointment to the witness. You spend time talking with a person and helping to guide her through an understanding of the gospel and then she makes a commitment that appears real, but later turns out to be half-hearted. You have a suspicion that she has gone along with you perhaps because she has been emotionally depressed, felt badly about herself, or was looking for something that would ease the guilt she was carrying about her lifestyle.

You can usually tell when this is happening a few weeks after the initial commitment to Jesus is made. You notice little or no effort on her part toward a lifestyle change. In your conversation she said that she understood what it meant to repent and turn away from sin, yet now she is still into the same sinful lifestyle. It can be frustrating to carefully explain the gospel, to dialogue with her about the claims of the gospel and the requirements for living the Christian life, and then to watch that person fail to change.

This happened to me with a person whom I counseled for a long time. I discussed the gospel with her at great length. She verbalized to me with great emotion her need for forgiveness of the sin of adultery in her life. She said to me that she realized that she was not a Christian and desired to become one. I carefully talked with her about the faith and she assured me that she was ready to confess Christ.

We prayed together, and she voiced a prayer of confession, repentance, and desire to become the Christian she knew she wanted to be. A few weeks later, she had had another affair. She was into the same lifestyle and apparently had not had the life-changing encounter with Christ that I thought she had.

In a situation like this it is necessary to confront the person and encourage them to evaluate their behavior. Have they seen that behavior as wrong and a contradiction to what they earlier had committed to? If not, why not? With a person who has come from a nonreligiously oriented background, you might understand the confusion and you will need to carefully explain the position of the Scripture on their lifestyle. But what about a person who has grown up in church and who engages in this kind of behavior? You may have someone on your hands who has a toxic understanding of the faith. In other words, they use faith as a crutch to get through life. When this happens the individual needs to receive help from a counselor who specializes in this problem. Support is still needed from the witness so that after the counseling is undertaken, the discipling process can be entered into and regular progress can be recorded as the person grows into the knowledge of what a personal commitment to Christ really means.

For many who are from cults, world religion backgrounds, or from a secular perspective on life, cautious trust may be the first step toward faith. The dialogical process of leading the person to trust Christ may produce tiny steps of faith at first. You must begin the process of discipleship de-

velopment with the person as quickly as possible and provide as much support as possible.

If the person is from a cult such as the Jehovah's Witnesses, for example, he risks being an outcast from his family if they are devoted Witnesses. He may decide after
careful discussion about the Christian faith and dialogue
with you that he is willing to trust Jesus, but in his heart there
is still much fear.

The key for the witness is to be available. Be available
when he hits the wall of rejection by his friends, family, or
colleagues. Be there to pray with him. Get him into a network of other believers who will support him in his new-
found faith. If you leave a cautious person alone to defend
himself in a new faith, he may become defeated, frustrated,
and quit. Be willing to walk with your new friend in the faith
until his steps grow strong enough for him to walk in confidence alone.

RICH YOUNG RULER

The final category is rejection—and rejection hurts.
None of us likes to fail, especially in matters of the faith. We
like to have success with the people we witness to because
we know that it is a matter of eternal consequence as well as
happiness here and now. But sometimes we will fail.

Apparently even Jesus failed with at least one person he
tried to enlist in the kingdom. The story of the rich young ruler is a sad one (Mark 10:17ff). He had so much potential, yet
this young man would not do the one thing that Jesus required for him to inherit eternal life. He loved his riches
more than he loved Jesus or the promise of eternal life. Many
today have a *Rich Young Ruler response.*

When you are talking with a person about the faith and
you are rejected, try to determine if you can continue the dialogue at a later time or if a different tact is needed. The only

way to know is to invest enough time in the person to know why he is rejecting you.

Recently I heard a pastor tell me that he had witnessed and talked to a young man who was living with a woman who was not his wife. He had dialogued with him about the biblical standard of marriage and of his need for Christ. The man rejected the pastor and told him that he did not feel anything was wrong with his life. He did not need Christ and he certainly did not need some kind of paper to sanctify his relationship with his girlfriend.

The pastor discussed the situation with the young man over the course of many weeks, but each time rejection occurred. Finally, the pastor told the young man, "I have talked with you about your need of Jesus and you will not listen. You have rejected me time and time again. Now I must tell you that I am going to ask God to deal with your life and to help you see the wrong in your life. I am going to pray for God to do something in your life that will cause you to receive His Son as your Savior and to get your life right before Him."

That same week, the young man was in a serious car accident. He was pinned in the car, though more scared than hurt. The words of the pastor echoed through his mind over and over again as the paramedics worked to free him from the wreckage. When he was carried to the hospital he immediately sent word to the pastor that God had answered the pastor's prayer and that he was ready to talk further.

You and I may never see that kind of ending to a situation of rejection. We will be like God. We will carry the hurt of that person's rejection, and we will be sorry that he has refused to receive Christ. But after we have done our best to listen sensitively to him and to dialogue in caring love with him about the faith, ultimately the response must lie with him. Sometimes people choose to remain lost rather than to be saved, in spite of all we do.

These are but a few of the possible responses that you may encounter. They represent some that I have encountered in my ministry of evangelism. Whatever response you encounter, keep your ear inclined toward God. He will lead you to react in appropriate ways. In all your ways acknowledge Him and He will direct your paths.

THINGS TO THINK ABOUT

1.   EXPLORE THE CONCEPTS.

Explore how you feel about the possibility of persons coming to Christ as a result of your witness. What about those who reject you? How do you think you will handle the kinds of response that you will likely encounter?

2.   SEARCH THE SCRIPTURES.

Examine how Jesus reacted with the rich young ruler. How did He handle those who believed?

3.   DISCUSS THE PRINCIPLES.

Discuss the need for discipleship and nurture of those who make the decision to trust Christ. Discuss also ways the group or a friend might suggest to deal with rejection. Be sure to point out that the person is rejecting the gospel and not the person in many cases. Talk about the differences.

4.   ACT ON WHAT YOU HAVE LEARNED.

Share your faith this week. Whatever response you receive, spend time with God talking about it with Him. Let God speak to you about the results you had. Then tell a friend what God said to you.

Chapter 11

HELPING OTHERS LEARN TO LISTEN

"He who listens to you listens to me."

Luke 10:16

William Abraham has said that in the early church one could be relatively sure that the verbal proclamation of the gospel would be intimately linked to the Christian community and to the other ministries of the church that were essential to the rebirth and growth of the new believer.[1] At the beginning of the book I spoke of the walls of separation between missions, ministry and evangelism. I said that they need to be overcome and that ministry and evangelism need to be united. I know of no better way than through the ministry of listening applied in everyday life.

---

1. William J. Abraham, *The Logic of Evangelism* (Grand Rapids: Eerdmans, 1989), 57.

Christians who want to tell the good news need to learn how to listen to people and to do so from the standpoint of ministry to them. All along in the process of listening to other persons and their needs, the ministry resources of the Christian community need to be applied.

LEARNING TO LISTEN

Helping Christians learn to listen to the lost so that ministry and witness can be applied will be a challenge that the whole church needs to get behind and commit itself to. Church members should be trained to learn how to respond to others as they listen. And they should be able to draw upon resources needed in order to continue the dialogue when needs are uncovered.

As training is offered in the art of listening and responding to others, several key points need to be kept in mind.

First, listening to others is not the same as giving advice. I have never met a person who did not have an opinion to give, if I would only ask for it. One of the quickest ways to miss what a person is trying to tell us about her life story is to fall prey to wanting to offer her advice on the way she should live after listening to her for only a few minutes.

Jesus is the only person in history who has ever been able to know a person's needs before He spoke them. Still He listened to others even when the needs were quite obvious. Jesus went out of His way to avoid imposing His power on people. For example, as Gerald Arbuckle pointed out, Jesus knew the sick man at the Pool of Bethesda.[2] He knew that he had been sick for decades, but Jesus still bothered to hear it from the man. He asked him, "Do you want to be well again?" He knew that the man wanted to be well, but Jesus

2. Gerald A. Arbuckle, *Earthing the Gospel* (Maryknoll: Orbis Books, 1990), 216.

did not start right away giving him advice on how he could be well. He waited for the person to verbalize his need.

When we jump to conclusions and give advice to people when we scarcely know them, we run the risk of missing all kinds of important data about their lives that would inform a more proper response once a better relationship is established and once the person has learned to trust us. Furthermore, to offer advice immediately upon listening to the person's concerns communicates that we are not patient enough to listen for as long as it takes to really get to know the person.

Second, the listening process can be hurt when we are too quick to console or comfort persons. For example, if a person begins to immediately spill out her hurts or concerns, we may want to put a bandage on all the hurts as soon as we can. Harold Stone has said that "telling a wife whose husband has just left her, 'I'm sure he'll come back,' or a person going into exploratory surgery, 'Everything is going to be just fine,' is not helpful. Most people reject such reassurances as insincere—they may even mumble inaudibly, 'How do *you* know?'"[3]

The problem that quick consolation presents is that the person may indeed find out that everything is *not* all right. And the witness will quickly loose credibility in the situation. It will be difficult to present the claims of Christ in a situation where mis-trust surfaces due to circumstances not working out.

A third issue in learning to listen is to avoid platitudes. Life is full of complex problems with few easy answers. Telling a person that Jesus loves him is a biblical truth, but it may be interpreted as a platitude by a lost person who is convinced that no one really loves him. It may hold no real value in his

---

3. Harold W. Stone, *The Caring Church* (Minneapolis: Fortress Press, 1991), 62.

mind. The listener needs to ferret out any such attitudes so that discussion and dialogue can occur around the biblical truths. The person's life may have been torment up to the point of dialogue with the witness. He may have been sexually abused by his earthly father, for example. To say the "Heavenly Father loves you" may present an issue that will need lots of discussion to be understood. The listener needs to be patient and to be specific with responses to all questions.

Listeners need to also remember a fourth principle. That is to use open-ended questions, and then to listen to the response. Don't put people on the spot. Instead let the discussion and dialogue flow naturally. "Are you saved?" is a closed-ended question. He can answer in a word: "Yes" or "No." Then the witness has to draw out from him how he knows he is saved or ask why not. That can be awkward. Some do not do it well. Asking a person what he thinks about having a personal relationship with Jesus, however, allows him to follow a pathway of thinking that informs the listener.

Robert Hughes informs a fifth principle that has to do with our nonverbal language. "Fully 55 percent of a message's impact is communicated via facial expression and body position."[4] Looking around when the person is talking, fiddling with papers, or looking up Scripture verses all tell the person you are listening to, "I've got a dozen other things to do more important than listening to you." Look the person in the eye when he is talking to you and he will feel your sincerity.

Sixth, the listener should avoid any verbal response that might cause a problem. An inappropriate laugh or negative comment can close the door to the conversation in a heartbeat. If the person is a nonreligiously oriented person and the Christian makes judgments such as "Christians shouldn't

---

4. Robert Don Hughes, *Talking to the World in Days to Come* (Nashville: Broadman Press, 1991), 125.

smoke" the conversation could be over, especially if that person is a smoker. It is a long journey for a secular lost person to get from a nonreligiously oriented lifestyle to where most church people live. Be patient with them, even when they say things that are strange or ask questions that seem out of place.

Seventh, the listener should be careful to remember that he is a layperson and not a trained therapist. Avoid any temptation to offer an opinion about a person's situation. There may be facts that have not come out in the dialogue, and the person may not have been entirely honest in the initial encounters with you. Remember, your job is to listen and to point the person to God. God is the counselor that we all need. He will speak to the person in ways that will meet the deepest psychological, spiritual, and emotional needs a person can have.

Eighth, the listener should seek to avoid any theological debate or argument. Dialogue should include answering the hardest questions that can be explored. But it should also include an openness on the part of the lost person to listen to your responses to his question. This will require trust on the part of the lost person that you are not trying to manipulate him, but that you are honestly seeking to help him discover answers to questions he may have had about God all his life.

Ninth, allow for cultural differences when you are listening to someone from another ethnic group, racial background, or religious tradition. Bear in mind that your own culture has colored many of your perspectives, so try to let the Scripture inform every response you make. Ask questions often to make sure that the other person is understanding as you dialogue.

Tenth, be available. Cultivate opportunities to listen to others. Begin thinking of lifestyle witnessing in terms of making new friends, listening to their perspectives on life, and being sensitive to the leadership of the Holy Spirit as you talk to people.

CLASSROOM INSTRUCTION

This book has been written to help interested persons do a better job of sharing the gospel through listening. As is often the case, many who read books on evangelism already have a keen interest in sharing their faith. And often they are leaders in their church in training and equipping others. If that is the case with you, the reader, this portion of the chapter will offer advice to help you develop further skills for your own listening and sharing, but it also will give a few hints on training others you would seek to mentor in the process.

If you are desiring to teach a class for persons interested in learning to share their faith, the following hints will need to be a part of the process.

First, communicate to the church, Bible study group, or interested persons that a class on evangelism will be taught that will emphasize the ministry of listening and dialogue throughout the process of sharing. Clarify with those interested that the class is not designed to teach another monological approach to the gospel presentation. Help them understand that it will be an inductive process and not a deductive approach.

Second, gather the group in homes or in an informal setting where people will be free to share ideas and be able to listen freely to each other. Host the gathering in your home and then pass the gathering place around within the group if it wishes to do so. Keep the group small enough to dialogue freely. Do not let anyone person dominate the conversation not even you, the leader. Plan to spend about three to six weeks discussing the book. Then meet once a month for three months for feedback and checkup. You may find it helpful to meet more often. In any case the time frames suggested are relative. Let your group decide what is best for the group.

When the group concludes the discussion of the book, encourage each person to pray for the Holy Spirit of God to guide them to a lost person with whom they can begin the process of dialogue and listening. Don't rush this process, but check up on the group often. Find out if each person has found someone with whom to begin sharing. You, as group leader, may need to be prepared to introduce someone in the group to a lost person if they do not know anyone who is lost. Many Christians do not know lost people because they spend their entire lives in the circles of Christian friends and church relations.

After each person in the group has selected someone with whom they are going to dialogue and to listen, begin the feedback sessions. The purpose of these sessions is to allow the group to get together and to discuss any problems encountered with the person with whom they are dialoguing. Suggestions and help from the group will be valuable. Keep the feedback group going for as long as the group feels is necessary. Celebrate victories. Pray together. Provide encouragement. Critique. Be honest and open in the feedback groups; otherwise the time will not be well used.

Third, in the three-to six-week training period, encourage discussion and dialogue. Lead the discussion freely through the fears of witnessing, the problems encountered when a prepackaged approach is tried universally, the problem of listening. Ask for testimonies as to the value of silence in the lives of those in the group. Other points of interest raised in the book can be discussed.

Fourth, make sure each member of the group has a New Testament they can mark to use as they discuss the gospel with their lost friend. Show them Scriptures using the Roman Road or another technique that you prefer. Provide witnessing tracts. Choose any of the popular tracts available that contain a good presentation of the gospel. But remember to emphasize that these tools are guides, and that dialogue and listening to the other person should direct the conversation so that she will understand every part of the presentation. You will want to make sure each person has these tools as resources as the dialogue moves along and as the two discuss the implications of salvation. Remember to emphasize that the use of the Roman Road or tracts or any other technique be done naturally within the dialogue and listening process.

Fifth, role play situations where dialogue is absolutely necessary to a presentation of the gospel. At the end of this section are listed some possible role-play situations. Use them for discussion and learning.

Sixth, as persons are led to faith in Christ, be sure that each member of the group becomes responsible for discipling them. There are many tools available in any Christian bookstore or denominational catalog.

Seventh, add to the group as persons leave the group. If a person leaves the group because he feels he has a handle on the process, encourage him to start a group. Multiply the groups. Add new people who hear about the process. Try to keep the cycle going.

Church Seminars

You may want to teach a mini-seminar in your church using the book. Take each chapter and outline it, present your own experience, and discuss the implications for evangelistic sharing with the group you are teaching. If you choose to teach the book and thereby equip others, a few hints might be helpful as you communicate the concept.

First, talk about negative attitudes and other obstacles toward witnessing. Help the group deal freely with the reasons why they don't witness or have trouble witnessing.

Second, talk about the dynamics of listening. Create some exercises of your own to illustrate your point. For example, ask the participants to look around and call out things they see in the classroom. Then ask them to close their eyes and call out things they missed with their eyes but "see" with their hearing. Be creative in order to illustrate the point.

Third, role play situations. Use the role play material at the end of this section in the book. The role play can not only improve the dialogue techniques of the group, but can point up holes in the sharing of gospel concepts. If there are problems with knowing how to properly share the gospel in response to the dialogue, suggest Scriptures and point them out to the group through the use of the Bible, evangelistic tracts, and other witnessing materials.

Fourth, emphasize that the class will be just another exercise if follow-up is not achieved by those wishing to learn. Develop some commitment cards for the class members to sign, pledging to establish meaningful relationships with the lost, and committing to dialogue with them, listen to them, and share the gospel with them in caring ways.

Fifth, from time to time ask for testimonies among those who are having success with the process. Debrief as often as possible in an informal way with the class members. Be an encourager. Be available to the class for subsequent questions and to offer helpful hints when they hit snags.

Sixth, use your imagination to develop other ways to train and motivate persons to listen and respond to the lost through meaningful dialogue. Examine books and other resources that you can find on the subject. Ask God to give you personal insight every time you listen to another person's life story, discuss life over coffee, or sit in silence with another. Seek God's presence whenever counseling another who is in the midst of struggles and difficulties or rejoicing over some achievement in life. Each time you find yourself with a listening ear, remember Jesus listened to the multitudes around

Him, and when He listened He responded with the good news. You and I need to listen like Jesus listened. He listened to tell.

ROLE-PLAY SUGGESTIONS

Copy each role play situation on a separate piece of paper. Give one part of the situation to a person in the group. Give the witnessing encounter portion to another person. Ask one person to act out the situation, to take on the character who is lost or needs ministry, and the other person to act out the part of the witness. Ask the group to observe the dialogue. Observe the dynamics of listening and silence. Ask the group to note how the gospel was presented within the situation. Have fun with the role play.

NUMBER 1

Scott is a successful manufacturer's representative for a national company. He travels a lot. He has a wife, Peggy, who is currently going back to school for her masters degree. A son and daughter also live in the family.

Because of the family's busy schedule, church has never been something the family had much time for. Scott and Peggy both graduated from the university and they like to go to the football games each weekend. In the spring and summer they usually spend each weekend at their lake home. It's the least they can do for themselves since they both work so hard.

Scott has remarked a number of times that he cannot understand why anyone can live in poverty. All it takes is hard work and a little personal sacrifice. His idea of God is that God takes care of those who take care of themselves.

WITNESS ENCOUNTER:

1. You have been given Scott and Peggy's name to visit. From what you have been told, they probably are not Christians.

2. Scott has been turned off once before in a witnessing encounter, so you may not get another chance to share the gospel with him.

3. You visit him on a Wednesday night, just after you have left your own church's prayer meeting.

NUMBER 2

Frank is a philosophy teacher at the local college. He has always had an interest in the philosophy of religion, but only from the standpoint of curiosity. He wonders why people place so much emphasis on a higher being. He is convinced there is nothing but the here and now.

Frank wrote his doctoral dissertation in philosophy. The title of his dissertation was "An Exploration into the Mythological Development of Deity in World Religions."

Frank's wife, Carol, was raised a devout Catholic. She and the children attend mass each Sunday. Frank spends most of his weekends working on his lawn. He says it gets him in touch with nature.

WITNESS ENCOUNTER:

1. It is Saturday morning. You are visiting the neighborhood, door-to-door, looking for prospects. Frank is in his yard. You and your partner decide to go up to Frank and talk to him.

2. You know very little about Frank, except his and his wife's name. You were able to get those names from a neighbor who knows them and who attends your church.

NUMBER 3

Betty is a biology teacher who has a blind son, Jimmy. She is a single mother. Her son's blindness was a result of venereal disease transmitted by her husband. Betty had no idea that her husband was unfaithful until she became pregnant and grew ill. She divorced him and sued him for support.

Betty is bitter. She keeps to herself and wonders why God permitted such a thing to happen to her. She had grown up in church and had always been faithful. Now she never attends. She stays at home with Jimmy. Even though he is blind, she has decided to give him the best of everything.

WITNESS ENCOUNTER:

1. Betty's name is given to you and your partner by a student who attends your church and has Betty as a teacher.

2. So far as you know, Betty has been away from church for ten years, the exact age of Jimmy.

NUMBER 4

Roy used to be a music director in a church, but he got his feelings hurt and dropped out. No one ministered to him; they just missed him.

Now Roy has cancer, but he is afraid he may not go to heaven. He believes that God has given him cancer because he dropped out of church. He is scared.

WITNESS ENCOUNTER:

1. Roy's best friend is a salesman. He visits Roy often. You are in the store where Roy's friend works and the conversation somehow gets focused on Roy.

Roy's friend knows you are a Christian and asks your help. He tells you Roy's story.

2. Roy's friend, the salesman, might have talked to Roy earlier about his fears, but he just didn't know how to witness in a situation like this. Besides, he is too emotional about the whole thing.

NUMBER 5

George is a mechanic. He has worked hard all his life but has never quite lived up to his wife's expectations. He joined the church when he was a boy, but religion for him never gave much joy. He always heard the preacher tell him how bad he was.

George never attends church now, but he is a good, moral man. He is visited prior to every revival and enjoys the visits but still remains indifferent.

Recently, he said to a fellow mechanic who happened to raise the subject of religion, "Pray for me that I can keep on being good, so one day I might go to heaven. I'm trying real hard to be a Christian."

WITNESS ENCOUNTER:

1. You wander into George's place of business. He recognizes you as the new preacher, even though he knows he never will attend.

2. You are happy to meet George. He tells you about his conversation with his friend.

3. George is obviously busy but you feel impressed to talk to him.

Things to Think About

1.   Explore the concepts.

Review the issues mentioned in the chapter. Why is it dangerous to speak in platitudes? When is it not always necessary to be quick to console? Be sure to work through these issues in your mind so that you will have a strong grasp of the principles.

2.   Search the Scriptures.

Try to find Scriptures that will support the issues mentioned. For example, how did Jesus communicate the gospel? In platitudes or in parables? In theological language or language of the day?

3.   Discuss the Principles.

How will the ten issues mentioned in the chapter directly affect your witnessing life? Discuss the implications with your small group or with a friend.

4.   Act on what you have learned.

Determine to share your faith using the information in the book. Then determine to gather some friends around you who will also put the book into their lifestyle. Teach the concepts. But most of all, let God guide you in every step of the process.

DATE DUE
